JUDY CREECH
3107 East 21st Street, Odessa, TX 79761-1813

Listening
For a God
Who Whispers

Listening
For a God
Who Whispers

A WOMAN'S DISCOVERY
OF QUIET UNDERSTANDING

PEGGY BENSON

GENEROUX NELSON
Nashville

Published in Nashville, Tennessee, by GENEROUX NELSON, *an imprint of Thomas Nelson Publishers (Nashville), and distributed in Canada by Lawson Falle, Ltd., Cambridge, Ontario.*

Design, typesetting & production by SCHATZ+SCHATZ. *This book was printed in the United States of America. To each of the craftspeople involved, our gratitude.*

The scripture quotation from Ephesians, found on page 75, is from Living Letters: The Paraphrased Epistles *by Kenneth Taylor. All other scripture quotations are from the Revised English Bible.*

Portions of this book appeared previously in "See you at the house.", *published by* GENEROUX NELSON.

Benson, Peggy.
    Listening for a God who whispers : a woman's discovery of
quiet understanding / Peggy Benson. —
        p. cm.
    ISBN 0-8407-7474-5
    1. Benson, Peggy. 2. Benson, Bob. 3. Nazarenes (Church of
the Nazarene)—United States—Biography. I. Title.
BX8699.N38B45   1991
289.9—dc20
[B]   91-4090
2   3   4   5   6   7—96   95   94   93   92   CIP

For Bo,
for everything

Acknowledgements

It takes a lot of people to make a book. Or at least it did to make this one.

It takes some folks to suggest that you should make a book in the first place. People who believe that you have something to say and are willing to help you say it. So to Bruce Barbour and the other people at Thomas Nelson Publishers, I say thank you for doing just that and more.

It takes some friends who are willing to encourage and stand beside you while you live through the times that it takes to live the story and to try and tell it. To list the names of Barbara, Carlana, Gloria, JoAnn, Joy, and Sue seems like not nearly enough to say thank you. To say what I really want to say about what they mean to me would take another book.

It takes a family who will hold you close and share their stories and their wisdom and their very lives. My mother, my father, my sister, my mother-in-law, my sister-in-law, my children, and my grandchildren have all done all of those things with great joy and care and energy and patience. I cannot imagine a life in these times or any other without them

It takes a writer. My son Robert tells me there is an actual difference between an author and a writer. According to him, an author is the one with a story to tell, a writer is the one with a set of pages to fill with words. Sometimes those are the same person, in this case, they were not. He is the one who took the note cards, the journal entries, the conversations on the phone and in the car and by the fire and in restaurants and on the beach and did what a writer does with them. He wrote and sweated and fussed and edited and cried and pushed and dug and made the story worth reading. Were it not for him, there would be no book. Were I to try and say more here, he wouldn't let me.

Finally, it takes some people who want to read the story once it is a book. Thank you for that, gentle reader, may you hear a whisper or two as you travel along.

Peggy Benson
Nashville
April, 1991

Prologue 1

No Talk Is Too Small 15

A Little Digging 41

It's Always Been Enough 65

Making A Home 73

Have Some Company 97

Summer People 117

Seeing My Children 125

Go to Church 143

Swap Some Stories 169

Go to Weddings 187

Epilogue 203

Prologue

*"Stop brooding
over the things that have passed.
I am about to do something new.
Can you not see it?"*

ISAIAH 43:18, 19

Nᴇᴀʀʟʏ ᴛʜʀᴇᴇ sᴘʀɪɴɢs had come and gone when my youngest son asked me if I could remember the sound. Not only could I remember it, I think I could still hear it.

He was talking about a sound we had heard on a windy, bright day as he and I had stood together, holding hands, occasionally blinking back the tears and other times letting them fall freely. The other children were spread out all around us across that little bit of hillside, holding on to each other and their wives and their friends and their children. I am sure they heard it too, but Patrick remembered that he and I had heard it together.

I told Patrick that I remembered the sound.

Indeed, for a long time afterward, I was convinced that the sound the coffin had made when it had dropped down into the vault would be the last sound that I would ever really hear.

On a day in spring, when the rest of the world seemed to be far away on some other hillside celebrating new life, we buried my husband.

ॐ

In the 35 years that we had been together, Bob Benson and I had fallen in love, gone away to seminary together, traipsed all over the country while he pastored in small churches, moved home to Nashville in the early sixties, cleared four acres of land along the lake and built a house, raised five children, had some grandchildren, struggled through all of the joy and pain of being a part of a successful family publishing business, involved ourselves in virtually everything that we could at our church, moved into the city to a condominium after the kids were gone, traipsed all over the country some more whenever someone wanted him to come and speak and would let me come and visit, and struggled with his cancer off and on for more than a dozen years.

He had been a pastor, a speaker, a writer, a father, a publisher, a business executive, a retreat leader, a retiree, a tour guide-in-chief on family vacations, a humorist, a gardener, and a storyteller.

I had been a wife, a mother, the lady in the

parsonage, an executive's wife, a traveling secretary, the keeper of the house, the director of entertaining, the head packer, a car pool driver, and the protector of the poet that lived at the top of the stairs.

We were a pretty good team.

He was shy, I never met a stranger. He nearly always kept things to himself, I was occasionally guilty of telling more than I knew. He was the financial planner, I was in charge of the spending division. He managed a business, I managed a household. He made the plans, I made them work. He made the major decisions, I made the minor ones. (Although we did have some pretty major discussions from time to time about what qualified as a major decision and what qualified as a minor one.)

We taught each other a lot of things in thirty-five years.

He taught me to lighten up about his illnesses, which were great and small and frequent. He used to say that if he knew anything at all, he knew how to be sick. People would ask him how he managed to cope with being sick so much of his life. With a twinkle in his eye, he would tell them that the first thing to learn about being ill is to never be sick without a stack of books. He was in and out of the hospital for surgery often enough that he even learned to make light of that too, though he was a self-confessed chicken about the idea of anyone, even a doctor he had confidence in, removing parts

7

of him.

I remember one Saturday morning, not long after he had returned home from one of the surgeries, that he told me at breakfast he thought he was feeling recovered enough to run over to the local Western Auto store to see if his "new parts" had come in yet.

I taught him how to celebrate anything and everything, early and often. At our house, we celebrated going off to school in the morning, and birthdays and "punkin" days, or any other holiday and the first buttercups of spring with roughly equal amounts of joy and fanfare. It seemed that no occasion was too small for calling forth friends and family, setting the big table in the dining room and the buffet table in the hall, and staying up too late, laughing and talking and carrying on.

He taught me to laugh at small calamities and to save my strength for the big stuff, I taught him how to make a home away from home when you have to be gone. He taught me to always be ready just in case a "moment" decided to land on us, I taught him how to gauge the caliber of any such moment by the volume of the giggles or the number of kleenex required to get through it.

At the end, he was trying to teach me that it was okay to live, and I was trying to teach him that it was okay to die.

❦

I used to think of Bob and I as a sort of package deal that God got when he got Bob. The arrangement worked fine over the years, right up until there were only two of us and not three of us anymore. Then it seemed to me that I was suddenly out of work.

The sound that Patrick and I heard as we stood there together beside the grave that day made it clear to me that the life I had shared with Bob was over. The sound rang in my ears for months after he was gone. It was loud enough to convince me that the rest of my life was already over as well, that I had lived all of the life that I was going to, that my life had stopped that day when the coffin slammed shut.

❦

We had always placed a pretty big premium on the things that we can learn from our children. Bob made a pretty good writing and speaking career out of telling the stories and sharing the lessons he learned about God's life and light and love from the everyday, common experiences of life. A good many of those stories and a good many of those lessons were ones that he discovered while watching and listening to the kids.

Not too long after his dad died, Patrick had gone off to finish his history studies at a pretty little school in the hills of Virginia. He came home pretty often, even though it took him almost six hours to wind his way through the wild, western Virginia hills, and cut through the haze and the steep climbs of the Smoky Mountains in east Tennessee, and come rolling through the countryside on into Nashville. He told me he really didn't mind the drive because he could turn his stereo off and think a lot about a lot of things on the way home.

It reminded me of Bob, but then a lot of things about Patrick the college student reminded me of Bob the college student. Quiet, shy, focused on his studies and his books and his reasons for being so far away from home, Patrick has the same boyish good looks, the surprising smile, the small frame, and the ambling gait Bob had as he moved across the campus at a pace that can best be described as intense meandering. If I were sitting under the right tree on most mornings at that little college in Virginia, I expect I'd be convinced it was Bob heading across the way to the library instead of Patrick. Or hovering along the back edge of a group of kids, not alone exactly, but almost, always. Young, handsome, intense, inward, that's Patrick. And it was his dad too.

Patrick was home from college one day, and he and I were talking about his dad. At the time, several of us were involved in collecting his father's stories into a new collection to be published, and I was asking him what the stories meant to him. We talked for a while about them, and then he said, "I don't really want to live in the memory of dad, but I do want to live in the hope and the love and the dream that he gave us. We can't recreate what we were, but we can create something new out of what we had."

🍂

Later on, I was bragging about Patrick and telling that story to his older brother Robert, and that got Robert and me to talking about Bob, and that got me thinking about another story. (I have a tendency to be that way. Even my stories have stories.)

I told Robert about how once toward the end I asked Bob if it was hard to die. He said, "No. It is only hard for a man to die if he only dies once."

Robert was very quiet for a few minutes, and then he said softly to me, "And it's hard for a person to live if they are only going to live once."

For a few weeks, I went around thinking how proud I was of Patrick for having learned such a lesson from his dad. And how wise I thought Robert had become while listening to his father. And, of course, how good their mother must have been to them and what a saint she was, bless her poor, sweet heart.

Later I realized that my two sons weren't talking to me about their father at all. They were talking to me about me.

❧

This is not a book about the dead, even though one of the principal characters of the story was buried in March, 1986. Someday, someone may tell the whole story of the life of Bob Benson, but for the time being, I am not the person and this is not the place.

And it is not a book full of conclusions either. Before I get to the end of it, it may sound like I have drawn some, but it will probably be as much about aspirations as it is anything else. Which is another way to say that it isn't as much about what I have learned as it is about what I am learning.

And finally, it is not a book about coping with death or grief or loss, written by a widow who has learned to cope with any or all of those things, though I cannot tell you the story of where I have been without talking about the one I was there with. My primary problem these days is to learn how to cope with life, not death, and so I leave all such questions to those who are far wiser than me. And to the Father, who has already defeated death anyway.

This is a book about the living.

And about the journey that one woman has been making to rediscover, reaffirm, and reclaim her place among their ranks.

No Talk
Is Too Small

*"I shall bless the Lord
who has given me counsel:
in the night he imparts wisdom
to my inmost being."*

PSALMS 16:7

W E WERE NEVER MUCH FOR RULES at our house. We had a few, but they were rarely discussed and even more rarely invoked. Bob was generally pretty good at keeping the few we had in his head, so that most of us who lived there had to guess what they were most of the time anyway.

One of the few rules that was clear as a bell was this: When the going gets tough, the not-so-tough also get going...preferably to the beach.

❦

Bob came from a long, distinguished line of family vacation-planners, and he was determined to do his part to keep the line of succession unbroken.

The longer the trip, the more family and friends involved, the more complicated the arrangements, the better he liked it. If getting away on a trip took more than four vehicles, or a foreign language dictionary, or a visit to the loan officer at the bank, it was his kind of trip.

In the early years at the publishing company, he had to travel a lot by himself. He would be gone for days at a time, riding the buses with recording artists, sitting up late talking after concerts, catching the red eye home to get back to the office as quickly as possible. He hated to be away from home, or so he said. Actually, he mostly hated to be away from home without any of us to be away from home with him. So as the years went by, and the business grew, and a new set of company executives came along to make the long trips across the country with the artists and writers and singers, most of his business trips were to retreats and conferences and conventions, and fell into the category of occasions suitable for family trips. Gradually the number of trips that he took alone grew smaller and smaller.

When the two youngest boys got old enough to be more interested in staying in town on the weekends to go out with their friends, Bob even bribed them into going with him by buying a round of dirt bikes and a truck to haul them in. If they would go with him, he would promise to go a day early and stay a day later, and find some trails they

could ride together.

And ever the helpful, supportive wife, of course, I could generally be counted on to throw a few things together in a few suitcases, and head for a place with room service with some token amount of persuasion.

When our children were younger, we used to go camping a great deal with a group of families in our church. We were all young family people, with great piles of kids and not-so-great piles of money. A couple of times a year, carefully scheduled to coincide with whenever the weather forecasters predicted buckets of rain, we would head off to some state park somewhere for a few days of wrestling with the kids under the cover of wet canvas. Inexplicably, it took me nearly ten years to make Bob understand that my idea of roughing it was a Holiday Inn without a pool. I think one of the key moments in the process was when we lost Mike in the woods for a few hours one rainy afternoon at a state park. Once Bob caught on, and once we had the money, he took us to some pretty good places.

One of our favorite places was Nantucket. Bob and I had first gone there on a weekend for just the two of us, and later we went back many times with family and friends.

You can fly to Nantucket from Boston, but if you do, you miss the best part of the trip. The best way to get to Nantucket, really get there, is to drive out from Boston in a car. All the way out the

highway from the city, the houses get more and more like the New England that is in your mind, and the wildness of the coast gets more apparent. On days when you are really lucky, the fog gets thicker as you drive along. Then you take the ferry across the sound in the fog, and your sweater gets damp, and your nose fills up with the sea air and salt smell. When you finally hit the island, you're hardly even surprised that in a little more than two hours you have somehow managed to sail your way pretty close to the nineteenth century. In fact, you are overjoyed.

The island is one of those places that holds sweet memories for us all. Most all of our children have some great story to tell about their favorite store on the island, or where they liked to walk through the town, or what great thing happened to them once when they were there. Their eyes light up and their faces start to shine when you mention the place, because the stories they remember from the island are so rich and powerful to them. Some of their father's favorite stories were from Nantucket as well. I suspect that heaven is a lot like Nantucket, or else Bob will have left a note on his mansion door as to where you might start looking for him.

A few months after Bob died, I was invited to go there with close friends who had gone with us before. Some of my best friends were going to be there and so were their kids. It was going to be a

great trip, a Bob Benson kind of trip, and I couldn't resist. To be honest, I was a little afraid to go without Bob this time, but then I was a little afraid not to go too. So I talked my oldest grandson, Rob, into heading off with me and I went. And it was a hard trip, just like I was afraid it was going to be.

Every day I would walk along the lighthouse beach and up through the town and over by the ice cream shop half-expecting to see Bob there, but I didn't find him. I would walk over to Main Street in the early morning, and look at the rows and rows of crates of fresh vegetables like the ones that we used to buy from together, and then go on up the hill past the bank and down one of the side streets and look at the houses that he loved, but he wasn't there, either. I didn't see him in the bike rental store by the wharf or up at the bookstore, or standing in line at the little theatre, or sitting out on a bench in the shade when I came out of an antique store.

I wasn't at all sure what he would say to me if I found him, but I knew what my question was going to be. "What am I going to do now?"

After a few days of keeping an eye out for him at every turn, I stumbled on how to find him.

I found that if I would close my eyes and listen to the stories he used to tell of Robin and The Cock-eyed Dove and the ferryboat and riding our bikes back across to the lee side of the island, he was there. If I would sit quietly near the harbor and listen to the sounds of the boats rocking in the waves, and listen to the sounds of children's voices in the wind while they were playing in the surf, and listen to the laughter of my good friends as they crowded around the dinner table at night with their children, I could hear him. And I could hear me and my kids and my life as well.

The secret was to listen.

Bob had spent his whole life trying to get people to listen for their life instead of look for it. To be aware of the sound and the rhythm of their life and the life around them, so that they could hear the voice of God gently speaking to them. To listen for the soft whispers and the gentle melodies that are woven into our lives in between and underneath the sounds that threaten to drown out those very lives.

❦

Bob used to try and tell me to listen a lot, but I didn't listen to him much when he did. I always thought that listening was an okay idea, but talking is really more my gift. In fact, talking is more like a way of life.

Among those whom I consider to be my friends, which by some accounts includes anyone I have known for any period longer than seven minutes, I am considered to be a world-class talker.

In a time when the idea of the designated driver is hailed as a bold, innovative concept in public service, I am tempted to remind people that for years now, whenever I have gone out to lunch with my best talking-over-lunch buddies, we have nearly always taken an extra person along with us. Over the years, we have given hundreds of free lunches to quiet people through our designated listener program.

My family can (and will at the slightest suggestion) attest to my devotion to the oft-maligned art of talking. I have been told that my son Tom recently entertained a small audience for most of an entire rainy beach day by simply walking around the house and quoting famous vacation Peggy-isms.

My children could also tell you about the hundreds of hours of discussions that I have freely given them about all of the decisions great and small in their lives. Countless hours of talk, diligently going over and over the same ground again and again, no matter the time of day or the size of the phone bill, long before the decision was to be made. Or even, and this is most helpful, long after the crisis was past and the decision had been made.

They would also tell you, as soon as they stopped giggling, about the time we were in Germany and I struck up a conversation with a man sitting next to us on the train.

It was all very friendly, all about our family and our trip, and he and I were having a great time.

He was smiling pleasantly as I chatted away the miles, and then I asked him a question. He looked quizzical and raised his hands, and said, "No English." Out of the corner of my eye, I noticed my family on the floor in various combinations of laughter and tears. It was apparent to me that they had been that way for quite a while. Undeterred by his response, I asked the question louder, several times as they tell it. Finally, between gasps for air, Leigh informed me, "Mother, it doesn't matter how loud you talk, he doesn't understand what you are saying."

One of Bob's favorite stories was about a group of ladies who were sharing a bit of what you might call "interesting news" with each other about someone they knew. One of the ladies said, "Well, now, my goodness, I didn't know that. Tell us more, tell us more." And the first lady said, "I'm sorry, I can't. I've already told you more than I heard." Bob used to tell that story sometimes when he was introducing me to a group of people that he was speaking to, and then he would wink or nod in my direction as though he actually thought that story was about me in some way. (And to make sure that I saw the twinkle in his eye.)

Actually, he knew full well that I knew how to keep secrets. Secrets are things you only tell one person at a time.

The truth is that one of the reasons he liked to take me along on speaking trips was that he hated meeting new people. Not because he disliked them, but because he was afraid he would have to make small talk with them. Standing on a stage and talking to a few hundred or even a few thousand people he didn't know didn't make him very nervous at all. Having to have lunch with any three of them always did. He just wasn't very good at small talk. My motto was and always has been: "No talk is too small for me."

❦

I told you all of those stories about me so that you would understand something very important about me: I am a talker. I am good, very good, at all kinds of talking. Barking out orders to children, passing on news to friends, telling stories about my kids to strangers in the grocery store, whispering in church, making plans for supper, and making telephone calls of all sorts and lengths to virtually anyone, anywhere, anytime. There are members of my family who contend that Eisenhower invaded France with fewer phone calls than it takes me to arrange for a family dinner.

Once you understand that I am such a talker, then you will have some idea of what I mean when I say that listening has never been one of my weaknesses. And you will begin to see just how radical it was for me to think about needing to listen to my life.

In fairness to myself, I used to be so busy that I could hardly be expected to stop to listen. Five kids, the PTA, the little league, the field trips, the shopping, the doctors' appointments, the trips to the airport, the hurry to get to church on time—all of those things take a fair amount of talking to manage and mother and muddle your way through. In a way, it seems very reasonable to me that all of them together would conspire against my ever having a quiet moment to think, much less listen.

I must also say in my defense that more than one of my children calls me nearly every day, and I have come to believe that they actually like to talk to their mother. (Okay, sometimes I find it helpful to encourage them to call by leaving messages on their answering machines if I haven't heard from them in a while. They're short messages.) And though we haven't always agreed about everything, I think that most of them feel like they can talk to me about most anything. At least they know I'll have something to say about it.

Any way you look at it, listening to my life for answers to my new set of questions seemed pretty radical to a person who was most comfortable talking her way through and over and around and inside and out of nearly everything.

So as I walked those bittersweet streets in Nantucket, I talked to myself and to God and to Bob and to my friends, and I said over and over and over again, "What am I going to do now?"

And the answer came back, "Listen. Just be quiet and listen."

❧

Though I hadn't always noticed, the sound of my life has always been full and rich. And beginning that day in Nantucket, and through days and nights alone in my house in Nashville, I began to try and listen to it.

I wasn't always really sure I was listening to my life, it often seemed as though I was just wallowing in the memories of the days that I had spent with Bob. It still seems that way to me sometimes, and I am sure that it seemed that way then to my family and friends. But I was trying to listen just the same.

One of the first things that I heard is that I need to learn how to make time for and make friends with silence.

Silence is not a sound that I remember much at all. When you have five kids, a busy husband, go to church with 1500 other people, travel fifteen or twenty times a year, go to three conventions a year, and are a world-class talker in your spare time, you don't run into silence very much.

In the first place, for a mother, silence is usually a sign of something wrong. One of the older kids is out too late, one of the little ones is upstairs and into something he shouldn't be, somebody has overslept and everybody is going to miss the bus. You know how such things go.

Silence was generally something that would be filled up as quickly as it came. I pretty much operated under the theory that if I didn't fill it up, somebody else would anyway, and it might as well be me.

Suffice it to say that silence is a little easier to come by at my house these days. Suddenly, the kids were all gone and with them had gone the constant noise of the ebb and flow of the lives of growing children. No more laughter and splashing in the bathtub from little ones, no more dueling stereos at the top of the stairs from older ones, no more of the crowded, noisy suppertimes that used to happen all the time. And then Bob was gone and so were the little jokes as we passed each other in the hall during the day, and the breakfast conversations, and the faraway bumping and whirring and shuffling noises that come from writers' studios. Even though they were quiet noises, they served to chase away the silence just the same. Gone too were the phone calls to arrange speaking engagements and make travel plans, the shuttling back and forth to mail out books and newsletters, the frequent conversations to help fend off visitors so that Bob could have time to study and write. Silence came pretty quickly once it finally came to my house.

I was a little afraid of it at first. (Okay, so I was a lot afraid of it at first.) Not only did it have all the qualities of a foreign language to me, I wasn't at all sure that I would like what it was saying to me. So I did what any world-class talker would do, I got on the phone early and often and filled up my house and my days and my silence with as much stuff and as many people as I could.

My friends would come by to check on me every few days or so, and if they didn't, I'd call them up to check on why in the world they hadn't been by to check up on me. I went to church just about every time they opened the doors. I even went to two churches there for a while, just in case the Methodists had some stuff going on the nights that were being left vacant by the Nazarenes. By Tuesday, I usually had a plan for my sister and myself for at least one night on the weekend. And if I didn't, I'd be going nuts. And after a while, I suspect I nearly drove her nuts.

And, of course, when all else failed, I did have my family. When you are the grandmother of twelve and you have one daughter and three sons in town, you can drum up a crowd for supper about anytime you want. A lot of times, you don't even have to get in a car and go to their house, they'll be happy for their kids to see some cousins and destroy someone else's house for a change. Busy young fathers and mothers are generally pretty easily persuaded by a supper that someone else will cook. A lot of times you don't even have to cook it, they'll be happy to come see you if you have the time to order it in.

31

I got to where in a good week, with just a few hours worth of intense telephone work on Monday morning, I could fill in most of the silence I could expect for the week. But somewhere in there, perhaps in between phone calls one day, I started hearing a voice say, "I thought you were going to listen."

"Well, I did that already, remember Nantucket? I listened real hard for three days or so. And besides, I can't right now, it's so noisy around here. And tomorrow, I'm going to..."

❦

I have finally come to understand that it is only in the silence that I can hear the story of my life and the voice of God talking to me through the telling of it.

If I will take the time to listen to my life, I can see where I have been and where I am going.

If I have the courage to listen to it, really listen to it, I can hear God speak to me about where I am now, not just about where I was back when my story was fresh and new and beginning.

If I will just be quiet and listen, I can hear him whisper to me about the story of my life that is being written this moment. About the needs and dreams and cares and joys and pains that were here an hour ago, and are going to be among the things I am going to need and want to remember and treasure in years to come.

❦

Sometimes when I am traveling and speaking, as opposed to just going and talking, I find myself telling people that they really need to learn to take the time to listen to their lives. That they need to make some room for silence in their lives, to not be afraid of it, to seek it out and cherish it as a way to bring healing to their tired and battered souls. And I just sound so pious and smart and good that it makes me nervous.

I catch myself thinking, "Do I really have any business saying that to people? People whose lives are so caught up in all of the good things that I was so caught up in not too many years ago. People who barely have the time to get all of the things done that they are responsible for. People who haven't had a meal without a bibbed person present in so long they can hardly remember what it is like. People who can't get alone period, much less get alone with God. Do I have a right to say such things when I did not even choose the silence in my own life?"

Now if it helps any, please know that this listening stuff isn't exactly something that I have mastered. One doesn't go from world-class talker to world-class listener overnight.

It was pretty easy for me to become a world-class talker. I suspect it had to do with a kind of natural talent for talking that I was born with. A gift, you might say. When I talk about the need to listen to our lives, I am talking to me as much as I am to you. And since I know the truth about me, and since now you know some of it too, I think I can just go ahead and say it: We need to learn to listen to our lives.

We have to figure out some ways and places and habits that bring us into some silence, silence that leads us into listening. Because God doesn't shout, he whispers.

After years of living in a house where the operative principle seemed to be "He who yells loudest is heard the clearest", the idea that God doesn't scream at us was pretty much news to me. I always figured that God must have shouted some, because there certainly didn't seem to be any other way to get heard at our house. But I am coming to believe that God doesn't shout or scream either one.

We like to think that God doesn't shout at us. What we aren't so sure about is what that means. Because it probably means that if we are going to hear him in our lives, we are going to have to listen for him in our lives. And that will likely take some time and energy, things we don't generally feel like we have enough of to spare.

More and more, I believe that he just quietly, patiently waits for us to stop and listen for his voice. It may well be that he is waiting for a day when we stop filling up our ears with so much other stuff all the time that we can listen with our hearts to what he has to say to us.

🦋

I am also beginning to think we need to be taking time to listen to our lives as they go past, because if we aren't careful, we'll miss our lives as they go past.

A few weeks after Bob died, I was talking with one of my really good friends. She and her husband have been close to our family for a long time. For nearly thirty years now, we have counted Bob and Joy MacKenzie among our great and good friends. We worked together and raised kids together and took trips together, and laughed and cried together through most all of the good times and the bad times and a better than average amount of the times in-between. We have watched each other's kids, and sat at each other's bedsides in hospital rooms, and fought over stuff, and made up over the same stuff, and prayed together over all the stuff for about half our lives now.

You know that kind of friends? Sometimes you can just tell when they are about to say something really important. When that's about to happen, you get quiet and listen. Even if you are me.

Not too many years ago, Joy had lost her mother, a great and funny lady who had lived this

kind of larger-than-life normal life, and Joy was
trying to tell me that the day would come when the
kids and I would sit around and tell Bob Benson
stories and just laugh and hoot and holler and have
such a good time. In the same way that she and her
sister and brother did that now about her mother,
Flo. She was sure that one day we would do the
same thing about Bob as well. Some of my kids were
standing there when Joy was telling me all this, but
they didn't look any more convinced about it than I
did.

But as time went by, we discovered that she
was right. The more we would tell the stories, the
more we would laugh and smile and feel close to
one another. The more we listened to those stories,
the more we felt in touch with ourselves and each
other. And the more we would look forward to the
times when the family could be together and talk
about the things that had happened all through our
lives. "Oh, tell the one about the umbrella...." "Do
you remember the time we played cards all night in
Canada...?" "The other day I got a note from
Robin...." "Do you remember when the truck broke
down in Kentucky...?"

One of the things that helped us along was the
collection of Bob's stories that we published. The
process of remembering them and reading them and
telling them and choosing them brought us face to
face with a lot of the memories and stories that Joy
had told us that we would someday come to revel

in, instead of shy away from.

One night, we were telling some of those kinds of stories at my house, and laughing and cutting up, and a slow realization began to dawn on me. That was my life we were talking about. My life was in those stories. But that wasn't the part that made me stop talking.

The part that made me suddenly become very quiet was this: In a curious way, it was as though I had actually missed a lot of those stories we were telling, even though I had been there. Because I had only seen them and hadn't really heard them.

All of us have moments when we start to get a sense that we aren't going to live forever. That we aren't going to get many more days than anybody else, and that we are going to have to come to grips with the fact that some day our life will be over. The fact that my life will be over some day doesn't really worry me much. What does worry me is that I will live one more day full of stories with my kids or grandkids or friends and not stop to listen to those stories to see what God might be saying to me through them and in them and around them.

There is one other thing I am coming to believe about the need to listen to our lives and the stories that make up our lives.

If we don't learn to listen to our lives, we may find ourselves without any stories to tell. And I am becoming more and more convinced each day of just how important our stories are to ourselves and to each other.

I am convinced that God speaks to us through our stories. It isn't the only way he speaks to us, but it is one of the most important and the most powerful. One of the most important things we can do is to listen to our lives for the stories that are in them, and to tell those stories as often as we can to each other and our children and our children's children. It is the way we pass on what we know about God's goodness and grace and faithfulness and love.

I'm not enough of a theologian or a thinker to know if I should be saying that his story is our story, or saying that our story is his story. I have to leave all that to the scholars and preachers and seminarians. But I do believe that somehow the two stories are inseparable, and that's what makes our stories true and worth the telling.

It is also what makes it important for us to be sure that we listen to our lives, to our children, and to each other. Ultimately, I think, it is how we will hear the whispering voice of God.

My "no talk is too small" motto has been true for me all my life. And it has served me well through the years. It has made me a lot of friends, enabled me to never meet a stranger, put me in line for a standing invitation to a lot of nice trips with a shy but good-looking speaker, helped to pleasantly pass the time in hundreds of airports and lobbies and restaurants and coffee shops and banquet halls, and earned me a distinctive place in our family's history.

What I hope and pray these days is that another motto might someday be just as true for me: "No whisper is too soft for me."

A Little Digging

"I am the true vine,
and my father is the Gardener."

JOHN 15:1

I SPENT THE BETTER PART of one summer muttering about mums. In between mutterings, I went to garden store after garden store, driving all over town with my teeth clenched, in search of some old gnarled-handed gardening wizard who could tell me how to keep the squirrels off of my porch and out of my pansies.

For most of my life, I have had a flower garden.

At the house by the lake, we had a big garden just down the hill from the house. It was stuck on the side of the hill and you had to stand sort of funny to work in it, the way you imagine that mountain goats must stand in order to keep from sliding off. We could have put it in a place that was level, but we were using the level spot for the house.

We had flower beds all around the house. They were nestled into the bottom part of the turnaround in the driveway and ran all along the brick sidewalk that led to the front door. There was a long, brick-lined bed that started just past the end of the house, and ran alongside the row of trees that stood beside the patio under the bay window in the living room. Down by the lake, there was a good-sized bed that wrapped around the little patio by the boat dock. The boys always thought there were too many flower beds because they had to drag the trim mower around four acres, but Bob and I thought that there were never enough.

The boys did seem to think that the flower beds made great end zones for football games, and that the big garden was helpful because it kept the basketball from rolling down the hill when someone missed a rebound on the dirt court that was just above the garden. Without a good stand of flowers there, one might have had to chase the ball all the way to the lake.

Just in case you think I am exaggerating a bit about the hill being steep, you should know that Tom once planted pumpkins there and kept losing them. We warned him that it wasn't such a good spot for planting them, but he had gotten the seeds from his teacher and he wanted them to be planted in the real garden. I can still remember his crestfallen, little boy face as he would come back in for breakfast after checking his harvest. "I lost another one this morning," he'd say, with the sort of resignation you'd expect from a farmer in the midwest during the dust bowl days.

Tom is really the one of our children that knows about growing plants and things. From the somewhat disappointing pumpkin crop, he went on to learn to love digging in the dirt almost as much as his father did, maybe more. For several years, he worked as a landscaper, one of the places he worked was in the development where my new place is. It wasn't exactly a chore for me to invite the tall, good-looking yard man in for lunch. I'd go to the door and call him and he'd say, "Okay, Peg," in the mischievous way he always calls my name.

Tom loves to do the kind of work you do with your hands. He's a carpenter now, learning how to do in earnest another of the things his father did for fun. Bob wrote a poem about Tom once, about the way that little boys follow their fathers around and do the same things their fathers do. At the end of the poem, Bob says that if Tom thinks his father is okay, then there must be something to his father after all. There is something to Tom too, something deep and rich and honest that comes to life when he takes up a simple tool to do a hard day's work in the sun.

Bob loved the garden. He loved to get up early and spend an hour or so in it before he had to get dressed and go off to town and into the office. And Saturdays never began early enough for him. He'd be up as soon as it was light, park himself underneath one of the funny old hats that the kids always laughed at, and be out making like a gentleman farmer long before the rest of the house came to life. When the property was so covered with woods and underbrush that you could hardly see the river when you were standing on the bank, he had helped to clear the land so that there would be room for a house and a yard and flower beds in the first place. He wasn't about to miss out on the good part.

When the older boys were old enough to drive the tractor and cut the grass, he usually rousted them out as early as he could as well. They were not very interested in yard work on Saturday or any other day, but a combination of vague threats about automobile privileges on Saturday night and outright bribes about water-skiing once the chores were done would usually be enough to get them going.

On most of those Saturday mornings, after the younger ones had been up for a bit and the sun was starting to get hot, my yard crew would come to the house for pancakes. I'd stand in the kitchen and keep making pancakes and passing them over the counter to the crew until they had enough to eat, and then they would head back out into the yard and into the sun.

Later, in the afternoon, I'd make a sweep

through the beds. I'd weed a little, move some things around, bark out orders to the crew for assistance whenever I needed it, get some new things in the ground, and set a sprinkler here and there. And then I would do what I thought was the best part, cut the flowers to take in the house.

We had company at our house pretty often, and they often said, "Oh, Peggy, what pretty flowers." I always beamed with pride.

❦

The summer I spent muttering about mums was the result of having chosen a place to live that was cool and shaded and quiet.

Bob and I had long since moved from the big house in the country to a smaller place in the suburbs, and then on to a little place in the city. We had just moved into a condominium when he got sick for the last time, and we hadn't really figured out what we were going to do about having a garden since we didn't have a yard to put one in. I never did figure out what to do about a garden there, because I didn't ever really live in the house myself. We weren't really in it long enough for it to seem like home in any way, so I wasn't very attached to it. It mostly reminded me of Bob's last few months, so I sold it pretty quickly and moved to another place a mile or two away.

A lot of people had told me not to do anything

too rash, too quickly. You know, something like sell my house and move, until I had some time to get used to all that had happened. It wasn't one of my listening days and so off I went. Turns out, I made the right choice, the new place is just perfect for me. Except for the part about the mums and the squirrels.

My new place is a little townhouse that is tucked back into the corner of a little development off a quiet street in a sleepy, older neighborhood. It is surrounded by huge old trees on two sides, trees that are right up against a fence that is overgrown with a thick hedge. It's green, cool, secluded, quiet, and thoroughly unsuitable for growing mums or any other flowering thing for that matter. Except for out on the porch.

Actually, the porch is a deck and it gets enough sun to grow things in planters and pots, like pansies for instance. It grows them well enough to attract the squirrels that live in the trees that provide the shade that kills everything else besides what the squirrels need for sport.

I miss having nasturtiums in the spring and mums in the fall and daisies in between. I miss the pansies and the geraniums and the marigolds and the iris. I miss looking out to see what new things are blooming and planning what new things you might put in over there in the corner now that the spring bulbs have died back. I miss having a place for planting the things that somebody is always

50

trying to give you some of in the spring and the fall when it is time to divide their plants. I miss the smell of the sprinklers and the sound of the scissors snipping flowers to take into the house.

I also miss having people say, "Oh, Peggy, what pretty flowers."

❦

Robert and I were driving somewhere together one afternoon and as we were riding along we got to talking about flowers and gardens and such.

I was muttering about my mums, or rather the lack of them, and he was gloating over his gladiolas. He mentioned that he had been out to the house by the lake just a few weeks before. He hadn't seen it in more than ten years, since the day we moved out, in fact. Which is a long time to go without seeing the place you called home. He had a lot to say about the house, but one of the things he said was that the new owners had let a lot of the gardens and flower beds go.

I sat there more than a little amused at the way he went through each bed, one at a time, and told what they had done to them, which trees had come down, which beds had been reshaped or taken out altogether, what kind of things had been planted to replace the things we used to have there. I hadn't expected that such memories and observations would come from a boy who had once vowed to have a concrete yard as soon as he escaped from the labor camp that he grew up in.

We went on talking about flowers and I told him that I had managed to get myself on the condominium association board long enough to help pass a rule that it was okay for folks to have flower beds in the common areas that happened to be in front of their townhouse. Tom was supposed to be digging me a new flower bed while we were gone.

When I told Robert that I needed to call Tom and remind him to put in some holes for iris or something, Robert laughed, though not unkindly.

"That's so funny," he said. "All those years, we dug the beds and carried the water hoses around front and spread the mulch and you got to cut the flowers and take the bow. Now Tom is going to dig the bed and you're going to get the flowers again."

❦

My job as "protector of the poet" was to make sure that Bob had plenty of quiet time to read and to study. He'd go off upstairs and I would take care of the phone and the door and all of the other interruptions. It was an okay deal with me, reading and studying were basically in the same group with listening as far as I was concerned, and so I was perfectly happy to be doing something else. He'd head up the stairs and I'd call out behind him, "Be sure and underline all the good parts for me."

It worked out pretty good over the years, with him upstairs reading and underlining and me downstairs running interference. He would be working on what he was going to say in the service tomorrow, while I would work on trying to get a group together for lunch afterward. He got to be the guru and I got to be the hostess. We used to laugh that he was in charge of the moments and I was in charge of the meatloaf. As long as we were together, neither of us went hungry for nourishment of either kind.

After Bob died, I got a call from an old friend who was the choir director in a church where Bob had gone to speak several times. I had gone with Bob, it was one of our favorite places to go. They loved him a lot, and me too, and every time we went it seemed like we were going to see family. They had been among the first people we had called when we knew that Bob was near the end.

"Could you come and speak to us at a retreat we are having?"

Before I could think about it much, I said yes and they said great and we hung up. In a few weeks, I started to try and think what I might say to them when I got there.

I went upstairs one afternoon to sit down and read and study and start to figure out what I might say to our old friends. I had spent a lot of years with a guy who was pretty good at this sort of thing, and I thought that I would just try to emulate what I

53

remembered him doing. After several fruitless attempts over several discouraging days, I began to realize that I didn't have much of a clue about digging.

❧

I am coming to believe that we have to learn to do our own digging for the truths that will shape our spirits. And I am also coming to believe that such a thing is pretty difficult for some of us.

But no matter how difficult it is, we must learn to carve out some holes in our schedules, some moments for study and prayer and spiritual nourishment beyond what happens to us in church, or else we will find ourselves with precious few tools to work with when it comes to growing ourselves or our children or our homes.

I have lived most all of my life pretty much convinced that time was the thing that kept me from spending much time in prayer and study. And it wasn't hard to think that and it wasn't hard to prove it to anybody. But I have to admit that I always found time to talk to my friends on the phone, read most of the magazines that came to the house, and study the catalogs in the mail.

I am afraid I am beginning to see that it wasn't that I didn't have the time, it was that I didn't have the heart.

I didn't ever really notice that about me

before. And I'm not sure that I much care for noticing it about me now. In the same way that the teenagers and the husband who dug the beds and hauled the dirt and laid out the hoses and carried the mulch and cut the grass, there had always been plenty of folks around to do my spiritual digging for me too, so that my spiritual life looked pretty good most of the time.

There was Bob, of course, and there were good pastors at our church. And there were all of our friends in the publishing business, authors and speakers and singers and songwriters who could be counted on to regularly show up with some fresh new things gathered up from the spiritual gardens they were working in.

Then there was the choir at our church and the Wednesday night services and the retreats and the college kids who hung around Bob, and it just seemed like there wasn't any need for me to do much digging on my own. I could just hang around and listen to them, they were doing so good at it.

ॐ

I have talked to enough other folks in my day to know that I am not the only one who has spent a good deal of time among the flowers in somebody else's garden. But I also am learning some other stuff too.

One of them is that you don't have to be very

good at digging before something will begin to bloom.

Robert has gone from dreaming about concrete yards to dreaming of the perfect year-round shade bed. He has taken a few square yards of dirt, the kind of "acreage" that comes with a condominium, and has managed to turn out some pretty good things.

I was out there one afternoon, looking at the flower beds before I went in to do what I really came to do, to see my grandkids. In the warm months, Robert has taken to meeting you as you get out of the car, walking you slowly along so that you have ample opportunity to see and brag on his flower beds. It's pretty good fun to see his flowers and remember that it wasn't so long ago that he couldn't even see the need for cutting the grass.

A garden tour isn't a bad way to meet Robert actually. It's more revealing if you can surprise him while he's working in it. He tends toward funny hats like the ones his dad wore in the garden. The kind of hats that his children will kid him about one day. He is patient, the way gardeners and writers have to be, and he takes great joy in a single flower and a single phrase. He rubs his beard when he is thinking and when he is listening, and he rubs his hands through his hair when he talking about some new flower bed or idea or project or other living thing he is working on. What he likes best is for you to get excited about it too, and for you to get down in the dirt and dig around a bit with him. He'll generally give you the credit if anything good comes in.

On this particular day, he pointed to a little bed of tall, willowy plants with feathery leaves and bright orange flowers that were glowing in the afternoon sun. They were beautiful. "Do you know what these are?" he asked. "Someone gave them to me and I don't know."

"They're poppies, I think," I muttered, knowing full well what they were. Specifically, they were poppies like the ones that I had tried to grow off and on for years without anywhere near the kind of success my concrete-yard son was obviously having.

But that's the way it is, isn't it? At least, that's the way it is with poppies and gladiolas and marigolds. And maybe with the flowers and fruits of the spirit as well.

Any one of us can do a little digging, be diligent enough with the watering can, keep an eye out for weeds and, with the help of the Gardener, we can begin to have a little something bloom in our lives. Something like patience or peace or discipline or love or joy. Something simple and beautiful, something that will shine in the golden sun of our days, something that will help us to take heart on the days when the storms come, something that may even cause a visiting friend to remark, "My, what pretty flowers."

We may not all grow poppies the first time out, or ever if my own experience tells me anything at all. But then again, Robert regularly looks a bit envious at the pots full of pansies on my steps at my house. He hasn't learned how to water things that are trying to live in pots yet. Perhaps I'll tell him, perhaps I'll just let him learn on his own. I'm still a bit miffed about the poppies.

❦

Robert's poppies and my pansies are teaching me something else as well.

I don't have to measure my garden by anyone else's garden at all. Which is pretty good news for a lady who has never been a speaker and who suddenly finds that she has been invited to come and speak.

I grew up in a time when the goal of most women was to be married and have children and stay home with them. I never thought of myself as an overachiever, but if those were the goals, then I certainly did my part.

I didn't go to college, didn't really learn to study, didn't ever really learn to love the search for knowledge.

I taught Sunday School class, but it was usually for a group of people somewhere between bibs and braces, so the digging required to get ready usually had more to do with getting doughnuts than it did with gaining insights.

I learned how to pray, but most of the prayers were said in a church service or in the dark beside a sick friend or a sleeping child. The other prayers I said were the kind you say in haste while you were standing over the ironing board or bending over the dishwasher or slinging sheets over the clothesline. I did some pretty serious praying about something while washing clothes in an old ringer washer once. It must have been something pretty serious, because I kind of lost track of what I was doing and got my arm caught in the ringer. I prayed over my arm too, once I got it out.

I was in a missionary group at church once, and one of our running jokes was that out of the thirty or so women in the group, only two of us were considered spiritual enough to open and close the meetings with prayer. I wasn't one of them.

I'm not unhappy or bitter or ashamed of any of this, but I do know that it left me feeling very insecure about digging around and trying to come up with spiritual flowers that anyone would think were worth looking at. And I know that that same insecurity in the face of all of the good stuff around, the work of writers and artists and scholars and preachers more talented than I, may well have kept me from picking up a shovel for a large part of my life.

What I have recently come to see is that this business of digging our gardens isn't about poppies or pansies or roses or nasturtiums or anything else we might grow. It isn't even necessarily about learning to dig up great spiritual truths that will dazzle anybody or get us nominated for sainthood. It's about discovering that we can and will bloom if we are willing to dig. It's about discovering that we are being called to grow and bloom as the seed that the Gardener has planted in us dictates.

Some of us will be tall and willowy and feathery and golden in the afternoon sun. Some of us will be short and dark and better suited to rainy days than sunny ones. Some of us will live our lives in pots on the back porch instead of in the big beds that are out by the driveway so that everyone passing by will see us.

But it takes all of us to make a garden. And all of us are as precious as a rose to the Gardener.

❦

What good news all of that is, isn't it?

Right up until about six o'clock on a Saturday morning when you don't want to get out of bed and dig. Or until the end of a long day when it's time to do a little reading or a little praying and you just don't feel like moving.

Or one morning, when for the sixth or seventh day in a row you pray all these powerful prayers, and begin to have a sneaking suspicion that they aren't being heard. Or one day when you hear the Lord tell you something that he wants you to do and you are too afraid or too lazy or too disobedient, and so you avoid him for a few days, hoping that by the time you get back around to him, he'll have forgotten.

❧

One of the first things I got for the deck at my new house was a Japanese maple tree. I put it in a huge, wooden bucket in the corner of the deck, just outside the dining room window so that I could keep an eye on it.

In the winter I put bags over it to keep it from freezing, in the summer I put an umbrella over it to keep it from getting burned up by the sun. I chased squirrels away from it, pruned it back carefully whenever it needed it, watered it by hand so that it would get just the right amount of water.

I could sit and look at it out my window and see what it was going to be when it grew up. Delicate, graceful, lovely, a tribute to my tender care and a sign of my graduation from the potted pansy to the sophisticated ornamental tree.

I came back from vacation this summer and it was dead. Brown, lifeless, barren, it was just gone. It was time to pull it out by the roots and throw it over the side of the deck to the trash bins down below.

The good news about digging is that you can actually have something grow. The bad news is that once you start, you can never stop.

Sometimes I think that's where too many of us decide that maybe it's just easier to live off of the fruits of someone else's garden instead of growing our own. And it may well be that the Gardener is going to be less than pleased when we tell him that we haven't been bearing any fruit because it was too much trouble.

🌰

In two or three days, Robert and I drove back to town from our trip. It had been a good trip, full of good talk and good folks and good times. But I was in a hurry to get home.

In the first place, I wanted to see if my most recent old gardener find was going to turn out to be a squirrel-chasing wizard after all. And to see if the pansies were going to turn up as flowers instead of food.

But I had something else on my mind as well. With any kind of luck at all, I could get to my house before Tom did, and dig my own holes for a change.

It's Always Been Enough

I do not busy myself
with great affairs
or things too marvellous for me.
But I am calm and quiet
like a weaned child
clinging to its mother.

PSALM 131: 1, 2

THE BEST TIME OF DAY to visit the harbor in Nantucket is actually at night.

In the daytime, it is a pretty place, but a mere shadow of the place it must have been when it was filled with the whaling ships and the men who sailed them and the women they left behind. The harbor is lined with new condos with widows walks, where it is unlikely that any widows have ever walked. The day sailers, tied up at the moorings with the nylon sails waiting for something less than real seafarers, are no match for the sailing ships of old.

But around nine or ten in the evening, when the moon is coming up out beyond the breakwater and the fog is rolling in, Nantucket Harbor seems to become itself again for a time. It becomes a magical and mystical place where the fog is so thick you can barely see your hand in front of your face.

The first thing you lose sight of when the fog comes in is the Lisbon light. There is a lighthouse out beyond the breakwater, and its light is the last light a sailor sees when he heads east, until he gets to Portugal. Those days in Nantucket, I felt a little like all the light I had known was behind me, that I had a long journey through the dark ahead of me.

After a while, after the Lisbon light is gone, the only real way to know the harbor is there is to listen for the sounds of the sea lapping against the hulls of the boats, and for the creak of the ropes as boats strain against the tide. You can tell that there are people around somewhere out there in the fog, because you can hear the tinkle of glasses and bits of laughter and talk echoing across the water. If you listen, you can "see" just fine.

❦

It was on a night like that that I began to hear, and listen to, the voice of the Father.

Now I don't really mean to suggest to you that it was the first or only time in my life that I had thought I had heard the voice of the Father speaking to me. But so much of the memory that I had of his speaking to me was wrapped up in the life I had led before. And as I began to face this new life I was to lead, I began to sense that I was going to have to hear him speak to me in such new ways that it was going to be as though I had never heard him before.

❧

"What am I going to do now?" was my question, over and over again.

"You are going to do the things you know," was the answer.

I checked off the list of the things that I had been doing all my life. Making a home, raising kids, having company, going to church, swapping stories with my friends, all the things that had been my life. None of them were things that I could ever do again in quite the same way.

I felt a little foolish, being here at the great crossroads of my life, seeking some great spiritual guidance, only to hear that I was supposed to be doing the things I had been doing all along. Except that now, of course, I couldn't do them. I could only look back at them, the way a young sailor might look back at the Lisbon light as he sails through the darkness.

"That's all?"

"It's always been enough for you, hasn't it? "

Making A Home

❦

*And I pray that Christ
will be more at home in your hearts.*

EPHESIANS 3:17

❦

SOMETIMES IT SEEMS AS THOUGH I was born making a home.

I've made them in all kinds of places, from Missouri to Florida to California to Florida again to Tennessee, with various combinations of children and pets and budgets and belongings.

I've made homes when I had a little money, and I've made homes when I had very little money, and I've made homes when I was somewhere in-between. Most of them were made when I was what you might call lower in-between. If no one has told you yet, you should know that homemaking is more fun when you have a little money, though it may not necessarily make you feel more at home.

Some of the places we called home were real winners. A pastor's wife doesn't need to learn how to be a creative homemaker because she has a lot of house to work with.

We lived in a garage for a while once. Though we hated to do it, the car stayed outside. For those who think we were being unfair to the car, you should know that we didn't own it. It was a loaner, and so it didn't seem fair to give it the "boys' room."

And we lived in a small house trailer. A very small house trailer. It was a vacation trailer, the kind that was meant for weekend family trips, not week-in and week-out family living. Living there was no picnic. Every once in a while, I pass a little silver Airstream on the highway somewhere and shiver.

For a while, we lived in a third-floor walkup with beautiful old hardwood floors that were lovely, but not level. Robert could get on his tricycle at one end of it and coast through the doors and down the hallway all the way to the kitchen at the other end without having to pedal. He also used to coast down the hill to the laundromat in the stroller while his pregnant mother ran along behind him trying to keep up. Unfortunately, he couldn't coast back home. The house did come with a live-in babysitter, though. One of Bob's seminary buddies, Champ Traylor, lived with us.

We lived in one large room in someone else's house once, and we lived in a duplex twice. For a while, we lived in three rooms in the back of a church. The good news was that we could walk to church, the bad news was that we had to be sure and make our beds on Sunday, because Sunday School was held in our "house." So was Vacation Bible School, NYPS, and the missionary society meetings.

Michael once escaped from the lady he sat with on Sunday mornings while his mother played the piano, so that he could go back into the "parsonage" to get a drink. To a three-year old, those little cups of grape juice looked more like a refreshment stand than a communion service, and so he helped himself to a few before he came wandering back. His father just sort of glared at him in mid-sermon, as he slowly came to grips with the meaning of the stain on his son's upper lip.

We lived in a brand new parsonage for a while, though not as long as we planned. Bob had to build a lot of it himself and so the construction was pretty slow. It did have a patio made of the broken pieces of concrete block that were left over from the construction.

What can you expect when you live with a pastor who had a church so small that it used to hold Sunday School classes in the back of one of the unrented U-Haul trucks in the lot next door to the church?

But later, when Bob's days as a publisher began, there was a big, fine home on the lake in the country. It was a place with a family room and a room for everybody to call their own and a living room to boot. It had a real brick patio by the living room, another one down by the lake, and a wooden porch by the driveway. It had lots of trees and a hill for climbing and woods to play in and enough room to grow a garden and a stand of pine trees and five children. It had company and Christmas and snowstorms and lawn parties and football games. It had love pouring in and out its windows, and memories etched into its rooms and laughter in its very walls. It was the home that was really home to all of us, the place where "Bob and Peggy and the kids" lived and loved and grew up and moved away from and came home to for twenty years. It is the place that I think of whenever I hear someone say, "Well, you can't go home again."

In my memory, it has become a great and magical and mystical place. In a way, I can't remember ever having not lived there, or ever having really lived anywhere else. Though I know the reasons, I can't imagine why we ever left it. And though I hate to say it, it was right to leave it, I can't imagine living there now without the ones who made it home for those twenty years. Whatever I learned about home, I really learned there I think, even though some of it I didn't know that I knew until long after I had gone from its sweet rooms.

After that, there was a great, rambling saltbox in the "good part of town." A somewhat clumsy attempt to downsize our lifestyle a little that actually turned into a wonderful surprise that we were later glad about. And then a little townhouse in the city for just the two of us after the kids had all gone.

All of them were home to me. Home has a good deal more to do with your heart than with your house.

❧

According to the Scriptures, it takes a chair, a bed, a table, and a lamp to make a home. Although I don't think of myself as a Biblical scholar, I am willing to hazard a guess that the writer of that particular passage was single, lived close enough to walk to the temple, and possibly had a scribe who came in to take dictation and drop off meals.

As one who mothered five, I can tell you right off that if you want to make a home for seven people, it's going to take a good deal more stuff. You are going to need two dozen chairs, six tables (one big one somewhere near the kitchen), a half dozen beds, not counting the ones in the attic that have been outgrown, and a minimum of ten lamps, more if you are raising boys who like to play basketball year-round, indoors or out. You'll need some couches with heavy duty springs in them, a collection of old sleeping bags for sleepovers, and a television that can be operated with pliers once the knobs come off. I recommend primitive antiques for large families, they come with knicks and scrapes already in them so you can't tell whether your family caused the damage or someone else's did long ago.

My experience is that you also need a large collection of books and toys and games and puzzles, a few thousand crayons, two sets of dishes (one for everyday and one for company), a good-sized collection of tupperware and other kitchen things, some rugs to trip over and slide on, and assorted boxes for packing away the things you have outgrown but can't bear to part with. You won't need to worry much about clothes and food and gasoline and cold medicine. Those things seem to come and go as with the tide, appearing and disappearing with their own rhythm and reason.

However, you will need a wall and some shelves and little end tables to hold pictures of the people you love and the people who live there and the people who don't come as often as they should anymore. And to hold the little pottery birds and sand dollars and sea shells and candlesticks and jars of bumblebees and flower pots and all the other little somethings that you collect along the way that remind you of places and people you can't imagine having made a home without.

Some folks put that last batch of things into a category known as knick-knacks, and can take them or leave them. But someone, somewhere, deep in my past, told me that those are the things that somehow conspire together to make a home a home. And I believed them. My children were in charge of knicks at my house, I was in charge of knacks. They did their part and I did mine.

❧

In fact, I don't even confine my knack for putting little knacks around a home to the house I live in. When I travel and finally land in a hotel room, with its basic home away from home bed, chair, lamp and table, the first thing I do is unpack the "home" I brought with me. It usually comes along in a little bag that will go under the seat or under my feet or somewhere nearby while I am in transit.

It has the few little necessities that I need to have with me in order to feel at home when I am away. A candle or two and some flowers when I can manage it, a pen and a notebook, a Bible, two or three of my favorite books, a little potpourri in a little glass something. Most of the time, there is a cassette tape or two of music that I like, and a seashell or two from my last trip, and a couple of magazines to spread out on the tables. Usually there isn't a lot of food, just some crackers and cheese and an apple and maybe one or two bottles of soda that I like, since they don't usually have what I like in the machine down the hall. I hardly ever take puzzles and games anymore since my kids are grown, but if there might be grandkids around, including my own, I might take one or two. I think of it as a survival kit of sorts.

I have taken a fair amount of grief about my travel habits over the years from my family and friends. Gloria Gaither says that when they took vacations with us, they just sort of resigned themselves to the fact that their girls would spend more time in my room than in theirs, because "Peggy has all this neat stuff in her room, a whole suitcase full."

Once my friend Barbara and I were headed off by car to Dallas to visit her daughter who was in school down there. We were all packed and ready to go when Bob came out from around the house to say goodbye. He was standing by the car door, watching me spread out my stuff all around the front seat and the floorboard—magazines, pillow, book, cracker box, new tapes bought for the trip, letters to read on the way down, and sewing to do. While he was waiting for me to finish so he could kiss me goodbye and head back to the garden, he said, "You know, Peg, Barbara has one of those new-fangled cars with those places in the back to put stuff. Trunks, I think they are called. You may want to put some things back there."

After five or ten minutes, with Bob and Barbara giggling at my efforts to get situated, I headed back into the house to get something I forgot.

When I returned, he was leaning against the hood of the car with his "I gotcha" grin on his face. Since I didn't remember having been got in the last few minutes, I assumed it was his standard "You are sure funny" look and kissed him goodbye again, ignoring him as best as I could. I opened the door to discover a pile of sticks and some bits of string and straw and dried mud in the floorboard on my side. "Well, I just thought that if you are going to build a nest...," he said.

❧

These days, people talk a lot about living more simply. They talk about how our possessions have come to possess us instead of the other way around. They talk a lot about having less, about making do with not as much, about cleaning the clutter out of their lives so that they can really live them again. They talk about the things we own as though they can somehow take away from the real life we are to live.

I understand what they are saying. One of the things that any mother looks forward to is the day when all her kids are gone, so she can get rid of all the clutter that seems to pile up everywhere, keeping a home, and maybe a life, from being the shining place that she always wanted it to be.

It is true that we can accumulate so much stuff, some of it just for the sake of accumulating it, that it loses all meaning for us, and we find ourself with things we didn't know we had and can't remember ever having wanted. From time to time, I still get a call from some friend or another who wants to know if I want to come and get some piece of furniture from their attic that I had asked if I could store there when we moved from our last big house into the little townhouse. Usually I can't even remember that I had put it there. I've done some over-collecting myself from time to time, more often than I care to admit, and I want to be sure that you know that I know that we have to be careful not to lose sight of the real things of life in the midst of the shopping trips.

But I have to tell you something else that I think I am hearing. It is that our things, the stuff we accumulate and later call clutter and clean around and step over and pack up to move from place to place, aren't all bad either. For if we are careful and a little bit lucky too, it is those things that can add color and memories and surprise and wonder to our lives and our stories. And occasionally, they can add life itself.

I read a book that Annie Dillard wrote about living the life of a writer. In it she talks about the simple, basic things she needs in order to be at home enough to write. She travels a lot more simply than I do, I can tell you that. Something along the lines of a certain ancient scholar, to be precise.

I liked the book so much that I read her

autobiography of her childhood and in it she talks a great deal about the house she grew up in. She talks about it in much the same way that I talk about the house I grew up in, and the way my children talk about the house they grew up in too.

When she does, she doesn't talk about a place with only a bed, a table, a chair, and a lamp. She talks about a place with music and dinner parties and doll houses. A place with a yard for playing baseball and a room of her own and shelves lined with the books that opened her mind and heart to the writer she would someday become.

It is too easy to simply dismiss the stuff of life as just stuff. And it may well be dangerous too.

❦

The time finally came for me to make a home for a very small crowd indeed. My kids were gone, my husband was gone, there was only me.

So I went looking for a place to call home. It was a hard thing to do. I wasn't at all sure about whether or not I could even make a new home, for me or for anyone else.

Before too very long, a place came and found me. A friend of ours was building some little townhomes in a place that wasn't too far from my friends and a reasonable percentage of my grandkids, and so I went to see it. I liked it a lot from the beginning and I was anxious to get started, and so I plunged right in.

Even for an accomplished nester such as myself, it was hard to get in the right frame of mind for making a home for so few. It almost seemed like I was making a home away from home, so to speak. It was quiet, almost too quiet to seem much like home for anybody. And the stuff I was packing up and moving into it, though precious to me in so many ways, seemed to cause me more pain than joy at the moment, and so I was approaching the whole thing with a kind of "Aw, who needs it?" attitude. Packing boxes will do that to you, I suspect.

"Who am I going to make a home for now?" I asked.

"For me and you," he said.

"But I don't know how to that, do I?"

"Yes, you do."

❧

"I will make my home in you," Jesus said to his friends gathered around that table with him at the last big dinner they had together, before he went out into the night and into the garden and into the day that he would be hung on a cross.

With all the homemaking I had done in my life, you would have thought that I would have latched onto those words a long time ago. You might have thought that I would have regarded them as highly as anything else in the scriptures.

But the truth is that I never really noticed them before.

Making a home and keeping it made takes a lot of time and energy. It took almost all of my life to get the hang of it. And it took all my energy, in a way. At my house, Bob was the poet, the speaker, the reader, the spiritual one. He would spend long hours studying, reading, listening, praying, and writing down the things that he heard. It was his personality that seemed most well-suited to building a home for the Lord in his heart.

My days were spent somewhere between the knicks and the knacks, between the making and the making up, between the collecting and the putting away, between the moving in and moving out. What would I have come to know about the Lord making a home in me, and when would I have come to know it?

❦

Last year, just before Christmas time, I spent a lot of time at home. It was unusual for me to be home so much just before the holidays, we world-class shoppers and talkers generally hit the streets with a vengeance that time of year. But grandmothers with broken legs are not the most mobile of creatures.

One Saturday morning in November, just after I had finished saying goodbye to the Tom Bensons, who were off to join the cousins and nieces and nephews and brothers and sisters up in the country to cut Christmas trees, I took a left turn off the counter of a kitchen that I was helping to paint and fell behind a refrigerator. At first I thought that the only thing I had fallen on was another grandmother, which was true because she was underneath me, but evidently I fell on my leg as well, because it turned out to be broken. When the kids got home that evening, they had Christmas trees. When I got home, I had steel pins.

So I spent a long time in my house, a long time every day, a good deal of it by myself. Kids would come and go, and friends too, bringing food and books and medicine and stories of the outside world and grandkids to play with the crutches, but by and large I was alone a lot. Which is not my normal condition.

And in the time I spent there, I spent a lot of it in a chair over in the corner by the window, reading and napping and talking on the phone and to myself some too. Sympathy is one of my favorite things, and like most folks, I'm not above asking for it, but I'm not telling you all this to get more of it. Not this time anyway.

But when you spend that much time at home, you think about home a lot. And on one of those cold days, while waiting for Christmas to come and the crutches to go, I realized that the Lord was right. I knew how to make a home for him. And that most of us do.

I am slowly coming to understand that if we know how to make a place for those who need rest and quiet, a place where people can recover from the hustle and bustle of the world and its wounds, then we can make a place for the Lord.

If we can make a place where memories can be found, again and again, where stories are told and retold, where the special moments of our lives are visited again and again, brought out of the closets and dusted off to put on the shelves and walls and end tables, then we can make a place where the Lord can remind us of the ways his grace has found us.

If we can live our lives in such a way that we can hardly bear to be apart from the things that remind us of home and the life and love that is there, if we can't go away without taking some of it with us, if we can't go to sleep in a faraway place without some evidence of the life that calls us back again, then we know something of what it means to be homesick for the Lord.

If we can make a place where flowers can grow and where they are treasured, where their fragrance can fill the air, where they can peek out at us and remind us that there is new life at work in the world, then we can make a place for the Lord and the new life that he came to bring to us.

"In the beginning was the Word. And the Word was with God and the Word was God. And all that came to be was alive with his life."

That great passage in the beginning of John's Gospel, the one that scholars say tells of the origins of the universe itself, tells me of the origins of the home that the Lord has made and can make within each of us. It tells me that wherever there is life, there he is. And it tells me that we who make homes for life to be lived in them can make a home for him as well. Not just as an unseen guest who drops by occasionally for coffee or Christmas or prayers or goodnight rituals with children. He can be part of the very fabric of the homes in which those things take place.

❦

When you come in the door of my little place, you have to make a choice as to where you want to go next.

If you turn left and head into the kitchen, you'll generally find the biggest crowd if there is anyone there at all. Or you can kind of lean right, go up the stairs, and wander your way in to the bedroom and the sitting room. Or you can head straight ahead down the hall toward the living room, you just sort of aim yourself at the fireplace and keep walking until you get warm, and then turn around and there's a chair.

If you are a grownup, the trip to the living room takes about twelve steps. If you are three, the average age of my local grandkids, it's about twenty-two steps more or less, depending on whether or not you stop at the tea cart that is parked just inside the front door.

It's a lovely tea cart that I found somewhere, sometime. And it has lovely things on it, including a silver tray with tea service and a set of beautiful pink and white antique cups and saucers that came from my Aunt Penny's house in Virginia. One of those treasures that you remind elderly relatives that you want someday each time you go for a visit, and that you cherish when the time finally comes that it becomes yours.

Most of the time, the tea cart looks like something out of a magazine. I keep a candle or two on it, and I try to keep them lit when I am home, and the light shimmers off the silver tray and through the candlesticks and over on to the glass beads in the bowl that I put flowers in when I can manage. I have a lace cloth that hangs off the edge, and a little crystal sugar and creamer that nestles up next to the tray as though the ancient silversmith and the crystal maker had worked side by side in some New England village somewhere.

I've never actually rolled the cart into the living room for high tea with the ladies that come to see me, I have never actually served high tea. The whole business, cart and tray and all, is one of those things that people collect, can't live without for some reason, and then forget that it's there except when someone says, "Oh, that's so pretty," or when it is time to dust.

At other times, the candles are dark, the glass beads don't glow, the little cups aren't quite on the saucers and the pitcher is missing, having been pressed into service for a game of "cooking" or some such thing. The little spoons aren't in their little cups and the sugar bowl is upside down. Grandkids know what to do with cups they can reach and spoons they can carry and pitchers that are empty. They think it looks pretty, but they also think it needs a little action to be real.

It used to make me more than a little perturbed when I would discover that the tea cart had been treated something less than graciously by a crowd of little cooks who were looking for props instead of beauty. It was similar to the feeling I get when I find that the sticky little hands that held the pitcher also had been used to mark the progress along the hallway that leads to the living room. I still am a little sticky about that, to be honest.

But when the pitcher is missing and the candles are blown out and the lace cloth is crooked and the glass beads are scattered, it is a sign that life has been there, in my home, because of and in spite of and in the midst of my protestations and plans and pink cups.

For one who would make a home, life is the only reason to make it. And life is the only way it becomes one.

And life, the kind that lives in our homes and our hearts, is where the Lord of life is always at home.

Have Some Company

And when he had sat down
with them at table,
he took bread and said the blessing;
he broke the bread and offered it to them.
Then their eyes were opened,
and they recognized him....

LUKE 24:30, 31

❦

In the way that all children see their grandfathers, I suppose my children have always seen my father as a man who was born to be a grandfather, and I suspect that I have too in a way. Perhaps it is because I presented him with a grandson when I was so young, perhaps it is because he looks the part. He is a little, dapper man with a thick, gray mustache and a warm smile and a deep, booming voice that seems to come from another, larger person deep down inside of him somewhere. He has a smile that he gives away most all the time even though his life has rarely, if ever, been easy. He has a fair-sized collection of hats, which he has worn regardless of the dictates of fashion down through the years, and one choir robe to wear on Sundays when he plays the organ in church, which he has done down through the years despite the up and down and good and bad of his life.

For practically forty years now, he has been Big Papa to my children, and now to their children, and he is Big Papa to me as well. Except when he is Wally, which he is to my boys, who remember him as the best babysitter they ever had when Bob and I had to travel on weekends.

When people think of Big Papa, they think of hugs and smiles and the little Lutheran church where the organist and the choir are up in the balcony and big pots of home-cooked turnip greens and hats worn with style. They think of the time he came to see them in the hospital, and the time he drove them across town for some reason or another, and the way you can hardly go anywhere without him seeing someone that he knows and who knows him. The things that my father does best have never been the kind of things that one could turn into money. They are the kind of things that people mean when they say, "Boy, if you could bottle that and sell it, then you'd really have something." But since you can't bottle it and can't sell it, the Big Papas of the world just keep giving it away, though they will have little to show for it in the end, unless one counts memories and friends and hugs and music and flowers among the treasures of life.

❦

My father had a theory that the family that messes up the house together cleans it up together. And when I was growing up, that's what we did every Saturday, all day. My mother usually worked on Saturdays, and that would leave my father and his daughters to attack the house and the yard.

He had a reward system to help things run along smoothly. If we could manage to get our beds made and our things picked up by a certain time, then we could go out into the garden and cut any flowers that we wanted and bring them into the house. If we could get the dusting finished by the next deadline, we got to arrange the flowers ourselves, in any container we wanted. It could be a real vase made of crystal or china, or an improvised one made of a coffee can or a pumpkin (in season), it was the arranger's choice. If we could hit the next deadline, we got to take the arrangements and place them on any table in any room to be on display until the flowers were gone or the next Saturday came.

With an incentive program like that, it wasn't very often that we missed out on the big reward for a day's chores well done, and so we got to get the good china down and get the good candlesticks out and make out place cards and set the table and light the candles for supper. When the weather was warm, and it generally was in the southern cities where we lived, supper was held on a screened porch on a big wrought-iron table with a glass top that reflected the light from the candles and the crystal and the smiles in the faces of his little girls. And the faces of his guests, for he generally had invited some in for supper on Saturday nights.

After supper there would be card games and coffee and grown up talk, with the New York Philharmonic playing on the radio in the background. Sometimes there were stories to be read, or songs to be sung with my father accompanying us on the piano.

My parents weren't wealthy by most standards. Unless one would measure it by the standards of the little girls who sat around the Saturday evening dinner table in the candlelight. China and crystal were terms that were used pretty loosely at our house, if the truth is told. And the big wrought-iron table wasn't really very big, it just seemed so because the porch was pretty small. The gardens were more or less a collection of beds that were squeezed onto a small lot in an old part of town that had long since ceased to be the best place to live, even back when I was young enough to live there.

But it was a fine place to learn about texture and tone, and arranging flowers and polishing the silver, and setting a table so it would shine like the stars in a summer night. It was a fine place to learn about how to greet people at the door with a hug and a smile, and how to pass them the bread and refill their water glass before it was empty, and take their things to the kitchen when it was time for coffee. It was a fine place to learn about the difference between having fine things and having fine times, between having supper and having company.

It was a place where little girls could learn about hospitality and color and music and manners and beauty and, ultimately, about home itself.

It is where I learned that home is the place where people say, "Come in, we're glad to see you." It is the place where I learned that home is the place where you always have a place at the table. The place where you are missed the most when your place is empty, no matter how long you have been away or what you went away for. It is, in the words of one writer, "the place where, when you have to go there, they have to take you in."

And if you are lucky, like I was, it is a place where there are shiny, bright moments and some cozy warm feelings and some china plate suppers on Saturday nights, even if the plates don't match. A place that has an essence to it, an almost tangible aroma that is somewhere between fresh flowers and the smell of a real apple pie baking in the oven.

Ultimately, my father taught me that a home is about welcome. I am coming to believe that the gospel is about the same thing.

❦

Sometimes when I describe the years when Bob and I were raising our family in the house by the lake, I start to see this image of the seven of us gathered around the big dinner table, having supper together. Bob is at one end of the table, I am at the other. The kids are circled around on either side, hair combed, napkins in their lap, clean shirts, bright smiles. It's a beautiful sight. And I believe it happened just that way at least twice. It may have happened that way every night at Ozzie & Harriet's house, but not at Bob and Peggy's. At least not very often.

For one thing, dinner with our five was more like a circus than anything else. A small circus where there wasn't enough budget for three rings, so all of the acts had to perform in the same tiny space.

The younger ones were busy doing what younger ones do at mealtime. Short walks around the table, standing in the chairs, trying to find new places to hide the vegetables when no one was looking, wandering down to the end of the table to whisper something in the ear of the one person you were trying to talk to since they couldn't get their attention any other way. Bob finally instituted the one-foot rule at our house for mealtimes. It was a simple rule really, but it helped: One foot on the floor at all times.

And someone was always missing. The older

ones were headed to practice whatever sport was in season, unless they had already been there and were on the way home. Which meant that one parent or another was likely driving the shuttle service, while the other one was setting the table or clearing the dishes. And that some one of us was always eating before or after the rest of us.

Bob's business helped to make mealtime interesting too, because it meant that sometimes Bob was there and sometimes he was not. And sometimes you had company for supper and sometimes you didn't. And sometimes you would know you were going to have company before you actually had company, and sometimes you didn't. Sometimes Bob came home with the company and sometimes he didn't. Someone would come in the house just in time for supper and you'd call through the hallway, "Hi, honey, supper's almost ready," only to discover that it wasn't Bob at all coming through the door, it was some writer or singer or producer or preacher Bob had invited for supper. They usually had talked to him in the past few minutes and had news of how long it would be before he'd be along in a few minutes to eat with them.

Then there were all the others who came for supper, the assorted girlfriends and boyfriends and relatives and buddies from the neighborhood. Leigh dated the captain of the football team for a while, and a goodly portion of the defense just sort of adopted us as their second training table. Michael's best friend, Matt, was a semi-permanent fixture at meals and vacations. He has nice folks and his mother is a great cook, I don't know why he didn't want to eat at their house.

Then there were the post-mealtime goodbyes. Some portion of us, if not all of us, was headed someplace after supper, to the ballgame or back downtown to church or back to the office. In the summer, it was back out into the yard to cut grass or swim in the lake or play in the woods before it was too dark. Or the visitor would head back to where they came from or where they were staying. We seldom had overnight guests until we built a guest house. A lot of our friends were afraid to sleep in rooms most recently occupied by teenaged boys. Most often, we would go off in several directions at once. One to study, one or two to go play, someone else into the car and off up the driveway to somewhere or another.

But occasionally, just for a few moments, there were bright smiles and laughter and tinkling glasses and polite partakers. With a glass-topped table and the New York Philharmonic, I could have been at Big Papa's house.

❧

It is fashionable these days, I think, to talk about the hectic pace of our lives as though it was some awful thing that borders on evil that we really think we are supposed to be rid of some way. It is true that the pace can take us away from families and homes so much that we have almost no time to really enjoy them. It is also true that it only seems to get worse. For all the busyness that I knew during the time I spent presiding over those mealtime circuses in the house by the lake, it was in many ways a slower time for us all. These days, more often than not, there are two jobs per household instead of just one. And in a lot of homes, even where there is only one job and fewer children to make demands on the days and the hours and the energy, there is often only one parent too.

The electronic wizardry that was supposed to give us more time, the car phones and beepers and fax machines and home computers, and all the other stuff you can't keep running, just keeps us running all the more. I have a theory that there is an inverse relationship between time and all such time-saving devices. The greater the technological advance, the smaller the actual amount of time saved. But I also want to tell you something else that I know about the hectic pace of the lives that we lead.

It is that somewhere in the comings and goings of friends and family, loved ones and neighbors, girlfriends and boyfriends, and fathers and sons and mothers and daughters, are the chances to say, "Come in. We are glad to see you. There is a place at the table for you. We've missed you. Tell us how you've been." The fact that people show up at all, whether they are invited or unexpected, says something about them. It says something about all of us.

It speaks of a deep need to be welcomed, to be in a place where there is a place for us, even if it is just for a few minutes or a few days or a few years. It speaks of our deep desire to be included, to share, to sit in a circle of some sort, and to laugh and talk and cry and break bread and tell stories and all the other things that one can do around a table that welcomes us and takes us in for a few moments before we have to say goodbye.

Even the goodbyes have meaning. If no one goes away, then they can't come home again.

❦

According to the Gospel of John, the first miracle that Jesus performed was one that had less to do with the coming of the kingdom than it did with keeping a good party going. It also seemed to have been his mother's idea. Another time, Jesus showed up for dinner at Matthew's house and something must have happened there, because the local religious leaders stayed mad about it for the rest of his life. You can be sure that Matthew never forgot it. To me, the best thing about the story of the disciples fishing all night together was that Jesus was cooking breakfast on the shore for them when they were finished. It turns out that the best news Zaccheus ever heard in his whole life was that Jesus was coming for dinner. In the quiet that comes after a meal well-shared among good friends, Peter was given the news that he, along with the rest of us, was to become the shepherd of the father's flock. At the end of a long journey, in a little room upstairs somewhere in a big city on a holiday weekend, Jesus had dinner with his friends and washed their feet and broke the bread and poured the wine and told them his secrets and said goodbye. Was it an accident that when he met the two men on the road to Emmaus that they didn't really know it was him until he broke the bread and passed it? If all those meals weren't important, the suppers, the wedding feasts, the drop-in visits to folks' houses, the campfire breakfasts, the last big meal on the last big trip together, why were they remembered for all those years? Why were those stories the ones that were repeated by the disciples who knew him and the ones who came after?

❦

It is probably a little dangerous to make too much of all those things. But no more so than it is to make too little of them.

Something about the gathering, the welcoming, the hosting, the sharing, the talking, the parting, and all of the other things that went with having dinner with Jesus was so important that no one who was there forgot it. Something in those acts is so profoundly and so simply holy that Jesus used such occasions to impart the most important news that he had to tell.

The Nashville contingent of the Bob Bensons once piled into a pile of cars and drove to Kansas to see Michael and Gwen. We went to see them for Christmas, because they couldn't come and see us that year. What with Christmas and so much company and Michael's new church, the one with the gym where the brothers could renew their old basketball rivalry, and so on, there was a lot to see and do and a lot to say to each other. But of all the things we did that week, the thing I remember the most is the way we ate together.

Michael, with the warm smile and the big heart and the laughing eyes, sat at the head of the table when he wasn't tooling around the kitchen doing his best to help Gwen help all of us feel comfortable. Time after time, we would all linger over the table, telling stories, making jokes, remembering the things that hold us together. Michael has always had a pastor's heart and it occurs to me now that one of the places you can see it most clearly is when you are sitting around the table with him. If I were a member of his church, I'd be trying to have dinner with Michael as often as I could.

I think it was no accident that it was in just

such places that Jesus told his disciples who he was and why he had come and where he was going and what they were supposed to do after he was gone. Those are the places where he was the servant, washing feet, cooking fish, breaking the bread, taking care of the wine, saying the prayers. Those were the times when he said you are welcome, to the food, to the fellowship, to the promise, to the good news that the Father has sent me to give to you.

Those were the places where he said to us that the gospel is about welcome.

ॐ

Having the circus come for dinner is kind of rare at my house now. Though it still happens some whenever there is a good reason to have the kids and their kids over for dinner or a birthday party or something. It's about a three-table idea these days, and there are so many little ones coming and going, and so many parents jumping up and down to check on their comings and goings that you can't even enforce the one-foot rule very well. Many is the time that when one of these affairs is over, and the last sleeping grandkid has been carried to the car, I close the door behind them and realize that I had a good portion of my kids at my house for three or four hours and hardly got to speak to any one of them.

So on the suggestion of my sister Bo, we started this custom of having "adults only" dinners for celebrating birthdays for my kids. If one of the grandkids is a year older, then we have one of the circus parties, so that everybody can share in the experience and feel a year older afterward too. But if it is one of those who is old enough to keep their napkin in their lap, then we get out the linen ones and have at it.

It's pretty good fun too. I get out the candles and the china and the crystal. I used to put the silver out too, before I got robbed one night while I was away on a trip. I put the glass beads and the little mirrored centerpiece out so they will catch the light from the candles. I get out the butter knives and buy some fresh flowers and make appetizers and shake up all the potpourri. Later on, the "guests" arrive (which is what you call it whenever your family comes to your house all dressed up) and there are smiles and hugs and little glasses of punch before dinner and good conversation. We have pretty packages all wrapped up and arranged on a table, and dessert with real whip cream and coffee in china cups, and tell all of the old stories plus the new ones we are breaking in. And afterward, we get out some board game or another and laugh a lot. Sometimes we have such a good time that when it is over you have the feeling that you have been in some holy place with some of God's favorite people. It's like hearing the gospel of welcome all over again. Or for the first time.

Sometimes when they are all gone, I go sit in the living room and have one more cup of coffee and listen to the New York Philharmonic. I have my father to thank for that.

Summer People

❦

If the Spirit
is the source of our life,
let the Spirit
also direct its course.

GALATIANS 5:25

❦

On Nantucket, the world is basically made up of three kinds of people.

There are the islanders, those whose homes and work and lives are there all year round. You can usually tell which ones they are pretty easily, they don't have to buy stonewashed jeans, the sea air pretty much takes care of that sort of thing for them. Their complexions are heartier and their smiles are too.

Then there are the summer people, the ones who are so named because they only come to Nantucket in the summertime. It is a curious fact that you can be one of the summer people regardless of whether you stay for a weekend or for the whole summer. The only qualification is that you spend at least one night. If you have been on the island before or if you stay for a long time, you can even begin to think of yourself as an islander. But in your heart, you know.

If you are one of the islanders or one of the summer people, then you get to think of yourself a little more highly than you do of the day people. The day people simply come over on the ferry to spend the day at the beach or in the shops or walking the streets. They actually do the same things the summer people do, they just sleep over on the mainland. It's tougher for them to forget that their lives are over there someplace.

The lives of the summer people are over there too, they just find it easier to pretend that they don't have to go back to them.

🐦

"Listen," he said. I recognized the voice at least.

"All of those things you have done in your life were about you, but more than that, they were about me. They were about life and life more abundant."

He seemed to be saying that it was time again for me to enter into the courts of praise, to enter into the places where families gather around a table, to enter into the company of strangers, into places where I have never been, into places for rest and for silence and for work, and that he would draw me unto himself.

"If you'll come with me, you'll see me. And you'll see you too."

❦

What I really wanted to do, of course, was to stay in Nantucket. It seemed a lot easier to get lost in its streets and shops, to disappear into the fog on one of the beaches or near the harbor, to keep going back to my little room in the house where we were staying and keep having supper with the friends who were gathered there.

Eventually even the summer people have to go down to the harbor and put their things on the ferry and head for home. When the boat sails, it's time to own up to the fact that our lives are over there someplace.

Seeing My Children

❦

"I made your name known to them,
and will make it known,
so that the love you had for me
may be in them...."

JOHN 17:26

❦

Like a lot of mothers, I used to have a pretty long "when the kids are gone" list.

I used to say that when the kids were grown up and gone away, I would clean out all of the closets, and they would be neat and orderly all the time. For a while there, it seemed as though Bob and I had operated on the principle that it was just as easy to move as it was to clean the closets.

I told myself that when the kids were gone, I would organize the pantry. Finally my husband retired and, one day when I wasn't looking and he wasn't writing, he did it for me. He had been a stock boy at a grocery while he was in seminary, and it turned out that for something like twenty-five years, he had wanted to arrange all the soup cans in alphabetical order and I hadn't known it.

I knew in my heart that I would finish all of the sewing projects that I had cut out over the years and never gotten around to. A lot of people didn't believe me, including my daughter who is still waiting on the Easter dress I was making for her to wear when she was eleven. The truth is that if you wait long enough, your daughter will outgrow the things anyway, whether or not you ever finish them. Cleverly, I chose a classic pattern, and if she ever has a daughter, I'm ready to be a hero some Easter.

I promised myself that I would sit down and eat a holiday meal that I had cooked while the rolls were still warm and the ice hadn't melted in the glasses. It has always seemed unreasonable to me that the one who was in the kitchen most of the day has to stay there when the guests arrive.

And then one day, I looked and the children were all gone. Oh, it took a while, they are spread out pretty good when it comes to ages. And a couple of them moved in and out a couple of times. But finally one day they were gone. Gone to their own homes and children and mortgages and car payments and shuttle schedules. Gone to their own lives and times, troubles and joys. And, I suspect, to their own list of things to do when the kids are grown.

After all those years of being their mom, which is not the same thing as being their mother, it was a little hard for me to let go of them. Okay, it was very hard for me to let go of them. I'm not sure yet that I could pass a test. Fortunately for me, no one has come up with one.

Letting go of my kids is about as natural to me as listening. And about as difficult.

❦

The whole idea of letting go of your kids is one that Bob and I wrestled with the whole time we were raising them.

His idea was that you couldn't hold on to them too tightly or else they couldn't grow. And he thought that we weren't supposed to hold on to them, but rather we were to just let go of them and let them become themselves. It was pretty fine and romantic stuff, laced with great quotes from people like Kahlil Gibran and punctuated with suggestions about considering the lilies of the field. It was also stuff that seemed to fit his easy going manner and his pretty well-developed non-confrontational style of conflict resolution.

For example, he wasn't very big on giving advice to the kids. He pretty firmly held that it was best to let the kids make their own choices about whatever it was they were wrestling through. Once after he was gone, one of the boys was going through a tough time and had a choice to make that he wasn't looking forward to, and he said, "I sure wish

Dad was around. I know he wouldn't have any answers about all this, but it would be good to hear a good, 'I don't know, what do you think you ought to do?'"

Letting go of them was definitely not my style. I am a worrier, a first-class worrier, in fact. I'm also a fixer. Whatever it is, my first instinct is to just wade right in and thrash it around a good bit to figure out what everybody ought to do about it to make everything all right again.

Which is easy to do when they are little, not so easy to do when they are older, and impossible to do when they are gone. It's not impossible to try when they are gone, but it gets less and less easy as the days go by. Most of them hardly check in with me anymore before they decide about anything.

☙

I have to make a confession.

One is that I'm still not very good at the letting go business. My kids will tell you that, and I have even gotten to the place where I am admitting it on a regular basis. I have even had a couple of days here lately when I have resisted the urge to go charging in, waving my mother flag in the midst of the battle, seeking to solve everything for all time with a flurry of phone calls or confrontations. Like all mothers everywhere, my defense is that the instinct to protect and defend your children dies hard, if it ever really dies at all.

It gets harder and harder for me to teach them about anything. What I have begun to hear these days is that if I will listen, my kids have a lot to teach me.

❦

Like most mothers and fathers, if you ask me about my kids, I will tell you a great host of stories about them, designed to leave you pretty much convinced that I have somehow, against all odds, managed to raise five practically perfect ones. I'd give you enough detail so that you could begin to see just how perfect our home and family was when they were growing up, how the sun never set on our house, and how the days all passed with joy and peace and laughter and warmth.

When I was through, I'd do my best to look humble, and you'd do your best not to feel somehow diminished in the face of such superior parenting, and I'd put away my photos and you'd head for home, certain that the world is somehow a better place because there are such fine children out there in the world. I'm sure it would be a blessing for us both. It just wouldn't be absolutely true. We could reverse the roles and it wouldn't be any truer, either.

Now don't get me wrong, I think my kids are five of the finest people on the planet, and I have a deep abiding sense that indeed the world is a little better place, or at least some corner of it is, because of them. But it isn't because all was sweetness and light at our house. They are a good group of folks, but they have had some hard times and seen some dark days, some of them of their own making. And in some of those dark days, Bob and I, parenting legends though we may be, did more to hurt than we did to help.

Together, our family has learned some things about dying and divorce, about winning and losing, about pain and depression, about failure and broken dreams, and about a lot of other stuff that can come crashing into the lives of children and into the life of a family. As a group, we've seen our fair share of hard choices and discouraging moments and tough times. I expect we'll see some more before it is all over. As much as I would like you to believe it, as much as I would like for it to have been true, we didn't live in Camelot any more than you do.

So when I look at my children, the lessons for me don't have much to do with how to raise successful kids or how to be a successful parent. I'm not even sure what the measurements are.

The lessons for me have to do with something much deeper and more powerful than that. They have to do with coming to see the way God can work if we can let go and let him.

❦

When Leigh walked down the aisle to be married, a little more than a year after her father died, one of her older brothers walked beside her to give her away, while another one waited in the front of the church to help perform the ceremony. The other two were ushering in the crowd.

Some of the kids have bought some land together and have plans to build houses and raise their kids there together someday. One of them is Leigh, and she and her husband decided that if they were going to have a farm, then they ought to have a pickup truck and so now they do. About the same time that they bought their truck, which our delicate daughter now drives back and forth to seminary and to the church where she works, Leigh had a birthday which somehow slipped past her brothers temporarily. (I said we celebrated early and often at our house, I should have added that sometimes we celebrate late as well.) When her brothers realized their mistake, they gave her the finest, and possibly the first, truck shower in our town. She has the fuzzy dice for her mirror to prove it.

One of my sons wrote me a letter once and added at the end, "Please kiss the children for me. It won't be long until the kisses become only hugs or handshakes. They are growing up on us." It was from Patrick, an unmarried college student at the time, thinking about his nieces and nephews.

The year we were making plans for Christmas

135

and got the word that Michael and Gwen and the kids wouldn't be able to come home for the holiday, his brothers and sister weren't very happy at all. It was his first Christmas at his new church and he really didn't feel as though he could be away. So the day after Christmas, we all went to Kansas by car to see Michael and Gwen. There were five carloads of us, and it took nine days, and we went through two snowstorms, and spent enough money to have bought the local Toys 'R Us in the process, but it was well worth it. It was one of the kids who suggested the adventure in the first place.

While we were there, Michael started showing his new motorcycle to his brothers, who were duly impressed. Someone overheard my mother say that she had "always wanted to ride one of those things." Her Christmas present was a ride on the motorcycle, and we have a home video that is available to anyone looking to challenge their grandmother to have a little fun in her old age.

When Patrick went off to college in Virginia, two of his brothers drove along with him, unpacking the van and hanging around with him until he got settled. They took him to the obligatory Sunday brunch on the last day at one of those restaurants that only parents that are taking their kids to college go to, and then they cried and told him how much they would miss him. They even reminded him not to forget to write his mother.

I talked to Robert one Monday morning and

asked him how his weekend was, and he said it was pretty good. He had run into Tom early Sunday morning before church and gotten a hug, listened to his sister preach and then was served communion by her in the little chapel service at the church, had looked through his Saturday mail when he got home and discovered an encouraging note from Michael that he hadn't seen, and finished the day picking up his kids at Patrick's, where they had spent the afternoon with Patrick and his little ones at the playground nearby.

By about any measurement, I'd have to say that my kids love each other, and some other folks too, and that something right has happened there.

❧

I was standing at the front door of my house with one of my kids late one evening. We had been saying goodbye to each other for about forty-five minutes or so, first in the kitchen, then into the foyer, finally with me standing in the doorway and them down on the sidewalk two steps below.

It had been a tough evening. One of the kids was having a hard time and all of us were concerned and worried (not just me). There had been lots of phone calls and lots of handwringing, and there was still lots of uncertainty about what was going to happen next. It was one of those times when I wanted to fix everything, but I couldn't, and neither could anyone else. It was pretty clear to most everyone that only time would help. And that even when time had done its work, what was going to be left over wasn't going to be easy or painless or pretty. I would have given just about anything or done just about anything if I thought it would have helped.

Finally, after the long hours of talking and wrestling through all the stuff over and over again, including the forty-five minutes worth of "just one more thing" at the doorway and down the steps, my kid looked up at me and said, "I don't think there's more you can do, Mother. Or that you should do, either. You'll have to let go and let them go on, wherever it is that the going takes them. You and Dad pretty much raised us on the principle that if you plant a few seeds, and then let go of your kids, and let them grow, then those seeds will turn into something good. It pretty much comes down to whether you believe that or not."

❧

We have to let go of our kids for our kids' sake. When they are young and bright and bursting with hope and promise. When they are wounded and hurting and lost and confused. When they are on top of the world and when they are about to go spinning off of it. We have to learn to help without holding on, to care without crowding, to nurture without knowing all the answers.

We have to let go of our kids for our own sakes too. Hanging on to them, fighting tooth and nail to keep clutching them to ourselves is just as debilitating to us spiritually as it is to them. The more we hold on tightly, the less room that we have to receive something new. Hands that are gripped too tightly around something can't catch any butterflies or pick any flowers or hug anybody.

It becomes an act of faith. Either we trust God to hear our prayers and watch over our children and be with them as they grow or we don't. Either we trust our kids or we don't, either we trust the processes of life or we don't. Either we are willing to live with our hands and hearts open to the will and mercy of God or we are not.

If it sounds like I am preaching a bit, maybe it is because I am. Into a mirror, mostly.

☙

It seems to be becoming a custom that no birthday party for one of my grandchildren is complete without a new board game for my children to play while the young ones are dismantling the home of the partygiver. The last one at my house was for a little boy who was two. The guest of honor actually went to sleep upstairs several hours before his parents and uncles and aunts finally gave up and declared that the party was over and went piling out of the house and into the night.

I stood there at my goodbye post in the doorway and watched them go that night too.

It's a pretty good show, watching them all hug and laugh and buckle babies in and pack away the mountains of stuff that it takes to take all those little ones anywhere for the evening. People kept getting in and out of cars, running over to kiss somebody else goodbye, making plans, saying "just one more thing."

I can remember nights when that was me carrying a sleeping one and laying them in the back seat. I can remember when they went to school and got married and got their first job. I can remember their Sunday best and their Saturday jeans and their wedding clothes. I have seen them laugh and heard them cry, I have watched them fight and make up and hold each other up in the rain and in the surf and in the midst of the struggles of life. I have listened to their questions and watched them find the answers to some of them.

"How can I let go of them?" I thought. "How can any of us let go of our children?"

How can we not?

Go to Church

❧

If then our common life in Christ
yields anything to stir the heart,
any consolation of love,
any participation in the Spirit,
any warmth of affection or compassion,
fill my cup of happiness
by thinking and feeling alike,
with the same love for one another
and a common attitude of mind.

PHILIPPIANS 2:1, 2

❧

THERE WERE ABOUT TWENTY OF THEM that came in to the sanctuary on Sunday morning. Twenty five and six year olds in their ruffled dresses and little boy suits, with their church bulletins and hair bows and cowlicks flying in the breeze, giggling and whispering and holding hands. There was a crowd of mothers and fathers riding herd on them as they all slipped in the side door of the sanctuary and made their way to a second row pew that had been reserved for them.

I recognized some of the little ones because they are the same ones that I see standing in the Asbury Choir. You may not be familiar with the Asbury Choir from West End United Methodist

Church in Nashville, Tennessee. It's a small group actually and they don't tour at all. The closest they get to making a road trip is the adventure involved in their moving from the robing room upstairs down the hallway and the steps and into the pew and onto the platform and back on the Sunday mornings that they sing. The only reason you may have heard of them is that one of their members is Jetta Beth Benson, one of my granddaughters. When I saw them come in on this Sunday morning though, I knew something was up, because they didn't have their white robes on.

The other face I recognized was that of the children's minister who led them in just after the sermon. As the senior minister made his way down the few steps from the pulpit, the children's minister made her way in the side door with the kids and mothers and fathers in tow.

She's a short woman, only a little taller than me. She has a woman's face, though you can still see the freckles that her daddy must have loved. She's young and this is her first job on the staff of a church. She'll be graduating from seminary soon by way of liberal arts and medical school. The way little children love her, it is apparent to me that she was born to be a mother and a children's minister and she is both.

I recognized her right off because she is my daughter.

❦

When I was Asbury Choir age, my parents took me to the First Church of the Nazarene at 510 Woodland Street in Nashville, Tennessee. Lately I've wished I had the date written down somewhere, or a copy of the bulletin from that Sunday morning service, though I likely wasn't paying much attention to it at the same time. Most everything that has ever happened to me since that Sunday morning was connected in some way, directly or indirectly, to that place and those people and that Sunday.

It's a big church, one of the biggest in the Nazarene denomination, one of the largest churches in the city. It was kind of a birthplace for the denomination, their first organizational meeting was held there, just a block or so away from the old Tulip Street Methodist Church from whence the "rebellion" that became the Nazarene church began. In fact, one of the leading figures of that church was a man named John T. Benson, my husband's grandfather. He was a pillar of the Tulip Street Church, right up until the day he resigned from the board. He walked through the elegant rooms of the church and out the big oak doors and down the street and around the corner, and threw in his lot with the holiness folks who were sitting on folding chairs in the sawdust under the tent a couple of hundred yards away. The sawdust was long gone by the time I arrived, but not the warmth of the services or the hearts of the people who gathered there.

My father played the organ in the church for a while. Later he left it to become the organist in a Lutheran church, but I stayed. It was home to me by then.

I was at First Church with my little sister Joan on the day she and I left it to ride home on the bus to go and help fix Sunday lunch with my favorite aunt who had come to visit. She was my only official aunt on my father's side, but if there had been another one or two, she still would have been the favorite. She was funny and bright and we loved for her to come to see us. We loved the food she cooked, but more than that we loved to help her fix it.

It was back to First Church that I went a few weeks later, after the accident that took Joan on our way home from the bus stop that day. I went back there, dragging my broken leg and carrying a broken heart. And those folks took me in all over again.

There was a song leader at First Church named John T. Benson, Jr. He was the son of the man from the Tulip Street Church, and the father of another Benson I got to know pretty well. I can still see him up on the platform, arms stretched out, head cocked to one side, with his songbook waving and his forever slightly rumpled coat waving a good bit too. He was the man who taught me to love the hymns and songs of the church. He was the one who started the summer camp meetings down at Ruskin Cave where I learned about altar calls and praying through.

Brother Benson, as I called him then, had two sons. One of them was quiet and shy, kind of studious and serious, except when he was mischievous and laughing. He came home from college one day and noticed that I was not exactly the same little girl he had seen around the church before. "Well, Peggy Siler, you've grown up," were his words as I recall, and he was right. Grown up enough to fall in love and make promises and dream dreams and start a family and other adventures. And so we did.

We started the adventure in that church, standing in the aisle one evening after a service. A few months later I walked down that same aisle on my father's arm, and walked back up that aisle on the arm of my new husband.

I walked the aisles of that church countless times in the next thirty-five years. I walked it with my kids in tow, kind of ran it actually, trying to find a seat before the service started on Sunday mornings. I walked it on the way to the front for baby dedications and baptisms and weddings of some of those same children. I traveled the aisles and hallways of that church three or four times a week. To be honest, we were there nearly every time the doors were open. No mean feat since we lived twenty miles away.

I taught Sunday School there, went with church kids on retreats and camping trips, helped friends plan weddings there, attended a fair number of funerals there, and met the saints and the sinners there and learned about the thin line that separates them. I went to missionary meetings there, met most of my friends there, and played vice-mother to most every kid in the youth group there, and cried at most of the weddings that were held there. I even helped redecorate the old place once or twice.

I went there when there was one building and later when there were five. I was there when there were five hundred members and when there were more than a thousand families. I was there when the church was growing and when it was sitting still.

I found the Lord there, or rather let the Lord find me there, and made enough trips back to be found again and again over the years, through dark days and bright ones, through good days and bad.

I was a little surprised one day when I realized that I didn't want to go back there.

❦

The people of First Church have loved me through most everything that has ever happened to me. Through the pain of losing my sister, through the days when I was far away from home in the places where Bob was in seminary or pastoring, through the raising of my family, through Bob's long twelve year struggle with cancer, through the dark days that came after he died.

They sat up and cried with me, prayed with me, laughed with me, and held me close to themselves and to the Lord. They took me into their homes when I didn't much want to go back to my empty one, they helped me pack up furniture and get through the holidays and took me out to dinner when I was lonely. They sent flowers and notes and ham sandwiches and comfort to me almost constantly.

I was sitting in a Sunday morning service there one day, when I realized that I couldn't be there among them anymore. I looked around at the familiar faces. Faces I had known for a long time, faces whose lines and features reminded me of most everything I had ever known. Faces of people that had been Christ to me, enough so that they had loved me into the kingdom in a way that most of them would have denied had you tried to give them the credit.

But I also had come to see that the faces that I loved and the familiar surroundings and traditions and movements were somehow working together to keep me from worshipping. While the congregation was gathering each Sunday "in rememberance of Him," I was gathering up to remember that which was lost.

❧

It wasn't very hard for me to find a new place to worship on Sunday mornings, I just followed some of my children.

Robert and Jetta had come back from their two years in Chicago and had looked for a new church themselves. Robert had been raised at First Church, and Jetta had come here from Indiana to attend Trevecca Nazarene College and had called First Church home as well. But they had gone to a Presbyterian church in Chicago, and had found themselves drawn to a more formal, liturgical worship service, and so had found their way to West End United Methodist Church.

Leigh followed them there and Patrick soon after. Bob and I went a couple of times before he died. The first time was when Jetta Beth was baptized. Another time happened to be the first Sunday of the month, the Sunday they have communion at West End. Robert was pretty much beside himself that day, wanting his father to "approve" of his new church, wanting us to see why the worship was so powerful to him. At the end of the service, we stood in the front, with the crowd filing out and the organist playing, and Robert turned to his dad with a "What did you think?" look on his face. In a soft voice, Bob said, "I believe that is what church is supposed to be like."

I figured that any church that comes

recommended by Bob, Robert, Leigh, and Patrick Benson was a pretty good place to start to look when I was ready to go to a new place for a while, and so I began to find myself heading off to West End on Sunday mornings. I have not been there too long, but long enough to be on speaking terms with the Asbury Choir.

❦

I have to tell you that it seemed very strange to me at first to go to church in a place where I didn't know anyone. People were friendly to me, the way good church people are to visitors on Sunday mornings. And it's a large church, with more than 2000 members, and so it has its share of traffic jams in the parking lot and crowds of people gathering up children from the nursery after the service, and all the other trappings that go with a large metropolitan church like the one I was used to. It has its fair share of old people who sit in the same pews and young children squirming in the pews in their Sunday best and high school kids passing notes up in the balcony. It even has a sound man in the back who occasionally has a little trouble with decibel levels. And because some of my children go there, it always has some babies for me to hug and some nursery workers who know me by my other given name, "Gran." What it didn't have for me was the great host of people that made the church a family for me. At least it didn't at first, and even now, not in the same way as First Church.

As time has gone by, in the tension drawn between a place too familiar for me to be able to worship just now and a place that was too new for me to be able to find community just yet, I discovered some things about going to church. I am grateful to them both.

❦

Virginia comes in to worship at West End about ten minutes until eleven most every Sunday. I think she comes on the bus that they send around the city to pick up older people who can't drive to church anymore. In her fine, tailored suit and her hat and gloves, always gloves, with her cane tapping along as she moves slowly across the front of the sanctuary, she cuts a striking figure. She must have been quite good-looking in her day, elegant and stylish. She still wears her hair long, in the way that some older ladies do, the ones who were beautiful when they were younger. My son-in-law Tommy calls her Bette Davis, and he's right about the resemblance.

I think Virginia can't hear very well because she never manages to hear the "I am saving that seat" that I stage-whisper whenever I have managed to land on the third pew on the left-hand side, the one she likes to sit in. She can't see very well either.

She has a patch over one eye, and she brings a huge magnifying glass that she uses to read the large-print version of the worship folder that she picks up on the way into the sanctuary. Before the service begins, she performs the same ritual that involves the worship folder, the magnifying glass, the hymnbook, and a pencil, the ritual where she carefully marks each page in the hymnal that she will need to follow along in the service. I was a little stunned the first time I saw her writing in the hymnal, after all those years of trying to keep my little ones from doing it.

She isn't terribly friendly and she doesn't talk much to anyone around her. Even an old talker like myself hasn't had much luck with her. But I haven't tried very hard though, she is a little intimidating. But then I don't think she comes to church to see any of us anyway.

Virginia comes out on Sunday mornings to worship. I don't know her well enough to vouch for how much praise or thanksgiving she brings with her, but I can vouch for the fact that she enters the the courts of praise each Sunday for worship and each Wednesday for the evening prayers as though it were life and breath to her. Whatever else goes on in Virginia's life, whatever other struggles and trials that are a part of her life, Virginia remembers the Sabbath and keeps it holy.

Virginia has reminded me of something that I knew a lot better a long time ago: Sunday is the

Lord's Day, not our day. It may be one of our favorite days, it may be our day of rest, our day for seeing our friends and picking up our grandkids at the nursery to take them out to lunch. It may be our day for taking a nap in the afternoon or slowly wandering through the Sunday paper or lying in the sun as well, but first and foremost, it is the Lord's Day.

It is a day for entering into the house of the Lord with praise, whether the floor has sawdust or carpet or flagstones. It is the day for offering up our praise and thanksgiving, for letting the music and the sacraments and the rituals and the prayers rain down on us until we remember his story, and why that story is the only one that we ever really tell.

❧

I never was a big fan of Sunday School. Perhaps it was because most of the classes I was ever in were full of children. They seemed to be primarily focused on seeing how long it would take them to mess up that perfectly lovely outfit that their dear mother had gotten up early to iron before church.

But when I got to West End, I didn't know anyone, so I figured a Sunday School class was one way to meet some folks. I was pretty confident that if I could ever get a few folks trapped in a room for a few minutes, I could talk my way into making some friends, and so I showed up. They also have free coffee on Sundays, and if you know where to look, and the fifth-graders haven't gotten to them yet, you can usually find a spare doughnut or two.

I wandered in and out of some different classes for a while. Jetta Beth said I could go to hers if I wanted to, and it was tempting because she's pretty good fun, but I passed. I went to a singles class for a while, but I didn't seem to fit in even though I met the basic qualification for membership. A lot of the other classes that were organized around demographics didn't seem to work for me either. You know the ones, young couples, semi-young couples, used to be young, married, used-to-be-married, going-to-be-married, I'll-be-darned-if-I'll-get-married, golden-agers.

One day I went to a class where they were having a pretty serious discussion about their own journeys, and I found my class. It turns out that these thirty or so folks had made an agreement between themselves. They had committed to reading the same devotional book each day, to spending the time in study and prayer each day that was required, and to coming back to the class each week to talk honestly and openly about the struggles and joys and everything else in between that had been a part of their inner journey that week. Later I found out that they had also promised to have some better than average parties, and to pray for each other a lot. And there was a kind of loose arrangement about hugging each other on sight and calling each other on the phone to check in as well.

I was looking for a Sunday School class, and I found the body of Christ.

If the church is anything, it is the group of folks who have promised to walk along beside each other on the journey. They are people who have promised to keep walking when it is dark and stormy, to keep singing songs and telling stories to each other to encourage the ones who are moving kind of slow or racing too far ahead. They are the people who have promised to keep saying prayers and handing out hugs and lifting each other up. The more I get to know the folks in the class, the more I come to see that we church folks are not going to ever answer all the questions for each other, solve all the mysteries of the faith for each other, or figure out some way to take care of all the difficulties for each other. Or any of the other things that churches are "supposed" to do, including make us like each other. What we church folks are going to do, if we are very careful and lucky and diligent, is the only thing we really can do, and that is to walk beside each other.

I believe I have known this all my life. The people at First Church taught it to me when they took me in, and when they held me close when my sister died, and when they watched over my courtship and marriage. They were teaching it to me when they cared for my children and honored my

husband and invited me in for Thanksgiving dinner
when I was too sad to stay in my own empty house.
They taught it to me at all those Sunday services
and weddings and funerals and Christmas cantatas
and retreats, and in all the sacraments and Sunday
nights at the altar. Through it all, they taught me
things about the church that I didn't even know that
I was learning.

In the days that we lived in the house by the
lake, Christmas Eve was a time for a big family
dinner, for getting the kids off to bed so that you
could have time to finish wrapping the things you
hadn't wrapped and putting together the things you
hadn't put together, and for making the sweet rolls
and setting the table for the crowd who would come
piling in when the happy morning came. You paid
attention to when midnight came, mostly so you
could tell how far behind you were, and how much
had to be done before you could lay down and go to
sleep. Christmas Eve isn't like that at my house
much anymore. You wouldn't believe me if I told
you that all of my packages were wrapped and you'd
be right, but I don't have to try and assemble
tricycles anymore or get a couple of dozen sweet
rolls ready to pop in the oven. But it doesn't seem
like Christmas Eve to me unless there's a dad under
the tree, muttering over a set of pliers and

instructions in the middle of the night. So the last few years, I have ended up sleeping on the couch or in Jetta Beth's bed at Robert's house.

But before I do, I go to church. I don't think it's because I'm getting anywhere near being holy. I think it may well be because I know that if I get to Robert's too soon, I will have to work on the toys. It may also be because it is beginning to feel like it isn't Christmas Eve unless I go to church.

West End is a big, rambling stone church with Gothic architecture. It has the high ceilings and the dark wood and the huge pipe organ that are characteristic of old cathedrals. It has a great wide center aisle that leads to a wide chancel area with a lectern to one side and a raised pulpit. On Sunday mornings, there are grand processionals and traditional liturgies and great moments of drama and pageantry that move me to worship in ways that are new to me.

On Christmas Eve, it is lit up with candles and two huge Christmas trees filled with white lights. It's crowded, full of people dressed in their holiday sweaters and holiday smiles, each holding the candle given to them at the door. The chancel furniture is dressed in poinsettias and greenery and the royal purple paraments of Advent. The choir enters in full processional, led by a minister carrying in the Christ candle, heralding the entry of the light of the world. There are triumphant carols and holy scriptures and a seasonal meditation from the minister. There is a moment when a minister brings the large lectern Bible down into the center aisle and holds it up while another reads the gospel, proclaiming it in the midst of the people. And there is communion, a long slow process for a thousand people who must make their way to the altar rail to kneel and be served, with all of us softly singing carols along with the choir. It isn't hard for it to feel like Christmas Eve in those moments.

This past year, as the communion was finished, I had just started to ready myself for the part where the candles held by the persons at the end of each pew are lit from the Christ candle, and the light is passed down the rows, from father to son, mother to daughter, friend to friend, sister to brother and so on, when I noticed a stirring on the chancel.

In silence, the ministers had taken up positions beside the tables and lectern and pulpit and had begun to ceremoniously remove the paraments, turning the deep purple over to reveal a glorious white and gold. No one said anything at all, there was only silence as a thousand of us, crowded into the Lord's house on a Christmas Eve to see if the Child would come again, watched the ministers. When it was done, the ministers moved into the aisles with the candles, marking the beginning of the movements that would send us out into the street, into our private worlds again.

For those who have grown up in churches

where such a thing is done, changing the paraments on Christmas Eve may not be a surprise. It may have been a long time since it struck you as powerful. But it was pretty powerful to me that night. In that moment I sensed that every celebration I had ever had had been blessed somehow. I somehow managed to see that a sense of celebration can be found in the simple things. That even the simplest things, like changing the cloths on a communion table can come to have a meaning and depth far beyond what looks to be there.

I should tell you that more and more, I am coming to believe that church is a place where we can learn something about making celebrations into acts of worship, into moments where we honor him by a simple act done with love and reverence and a sense of his presence.

The children who came into the service on that Sunday morning were part of a worship readiness class at the church. It's my daughter's job as children's minister to lead the children, along with their parents, through a six-week class to help get the little ones ready to go to "big church" every Sunday, instead of staying downstairs in one of the classrooms. Although I suspect that more than a little bit of worship readiness has to do with when to sit still and when to stand and when not to stand on the pew so you can see better, Leigh tells me that a lot of it has to do with trying to explain to little children exactly what is going on in big church. Each Sunday, they meet in a classroom for a while together and talk about one part of the service or another, and then they come downstairs and into the sanctuary to participate, and then go back to talk about what they saw and did. And to get the cookies they earn for having been so grown up for those few minutes.

There is a lot to explain about a church service. Why they carry the candle in each Sunday at the front of the long line of ministers and singers, and why no one ever gets to blow it out. Why we stand to sing and sit down to pray, and why the minister puts water on babies' heads, and why a minister reads the Bible out loud when we all have one in front of us. Why we put the money in the offering plate, and why those people take it up to the big table up front while we stand and sing. Why that man talks so long, and why we can't talk when he does. It's a lot to learn and it can take a lifetime to learn it. Since this particular church is so new to me and so different from the one I have always known, I've wanted to go through the class myself, but I'm embarrassed to ask Leigh if I can. The real qualification for getting into the class is to have a little one and if it comes to that, I think I'll just muddle along without knowing.

On that Sunday, in between the time that

Leigh led her troop in and the time that she led them out, they took communion. They sat quietly, well almost quietly, while the minister said the great prayer of thanksgiving and we stood and sang the responses. They watched as he took the bread and then broke it and held it up for all of us to see, and they watched as he lifted the cup and proclaimed it as the blood of Christ. They watched him give the bread and wine to the ministers standing in the circle around him, the ones who would serve all of us when our turn came. They watched as the choir and then row after row of worshippers made their way to the altar and then knelt to take communion. Finally it was their turn. I was sitting in the transcept that Sunday, the section on the side that you end up in when you are late to church and are too embarrassed to walk across the front to where you usually sit. There are some disadvantages to those seats, but on this Sunday I discovered an advantage to them as well. I could see their faces as they came to kneel for communion, little hands outstretched, faces turned up to the ministers who offered them the bread and then a little cup.

I don't know how much they really understood about it all that morning. One little girl took two of the empty cups home with her "For Bert and Ernie," she whispered to her mother, "for their tea party." But I don't know how much I understand about it all, for that matter.

I can't explain everything about what goes on in churches. But I can tell you that the people who go to them are different than people who don't. I can tell you that the things that happen there can change your life forever, in ways that you don't understand at the time, if you ever understand them at all. I can tell you that if you will let them, the people who are there will lift you up and carry you along and walk beside you.

And I can tell you that if you will come to the house of the Lord, ready and willing to hear his story and to walk among his people, there will be times you will hear his voice.

Swap Some Stories

❦

They are to do good
and to be rich in well-doing,
to be ready to give generously
and to share with others,
and so acquire a treasure
which will form a good foundation
for the future.
Then they will grasp the life
which is life indeed.

1 TIMOTHY 6:18, 19

❦

My CHILDREN TEASE ME about the way I tell stories. I think it comes from the fact that my stories seem to have stories. I choose to think of this ability to move from one story to the next without necessarily having to finish one as a special gift for free association given only to mothers, grandfathers, and World War II veterans, but perhaps I'm wrong.

They also tease me about the number of times I say, "Do you remember the time that...?" and then tell one of our stories again. They always remember and they always say so, and I always ignore them and tell the story again anyway. The truth is that they do it quite a bit themselves. They just have the advantage of being younger and being able to

173

remember if they have already told that story to me this week or not.

My friend Barbara and I walk in the morning for exercise. Actually we walk in the morning for muffins. There is a shop close to my house that we go into after our walk to buy coffee and muffins to reward ourselves for being virtuous enough to get out and walk. It's a pretty good hike over there, but then it's a better than average muffin.

The other day, Barbara was telling me a story and she noticed that I wasn't listening. "Peggy," she said with a bit of indignation in her voice, "You're not even listening to me."

"Well, you told me that story yesterday," I replied.

She started laughing, pretty hard now that I think of it. "Well, so what, I listened yesterday morning when you told me the same story three times." It should be noted, for the record, that neither one of us could remember the end of the story in question.

Since then, we have instituted the "I've heard this recently and I'm not in the mood to hear it again quite so soon" rule for our conversations. It is pretty much in effect at all times, except for times of great crisis when you need to repeat things, or when we have a designated listener present.

Everybody ought to have some friends like that to swap stories with.

❧

After I had started to adjust a little bit to the new way that I was living, I decided that I would try and get a job.

I grew up in the days when most of the goals of most women had to do with husbands and a home and families, and since that set of choices was okay by me, I never really had much of a chance to prove to myself that I could actually get a job and function in the "real world." So it seemed important to me to do just that. I got a job doing something I had been doing since I was a little girl, arranging flowers.

Not too far from my house, there is a little shop that makes some of the most beautiful arrangements in our town. Bo knew the people who owned it because of the business that she is in, planning special events and conventions and business meetings. She has worked with the people in the shop quite a bit. I knew the shop because I used to go in there to buy a lot more than I should. Bo's thought was that if anyone knew anything about how to get people like me to spend a good deal of money in that store, it was me. She suggested that I talk to them about a job and they took me in.

But after a while, I seemed to have spent all of the time that I wanted to behind the counter in a flower shop. Maybe it was because I spent most of my time way behind the counter, way back in the back room, to be exact. I was in the back making flower arrangements a good deal more than I was out front meeting the customers.

It didn't surprise anyone who knows me that it was hard for me to go from a life of constantly meeting new people and talking with them about what is going on in their life these days to a life in a back room snipping flowers for arrangements that I never got to see on the table or for parties that I never got get invited to.

In a way, what I missed was being with people. But what I really missed was the stories they tell.

❧

I have a lot of friends I swap stories with.

I've got some people I call friends that are the kind of friends that you make just because they live next door or across the street. The folks with whom you trade favors like picking up the mail, or feeding the cat, or watering the plants for each other when one of you is out of town.

I've got some friends that I know mostly because we are working on some sort of project together. They are the people that one gets thrown in with because of some committee or some work project at church or some such thing. It's a relationship that is built around something you do together, and once you have done the work, you are always friends in a way.

I have some friends I have known for years and years, though I haven't seen them in years and years. People I knew from seminary days or when we were pastoring or in the publishing business. People that it seems like I have always known and always will because of what we shared together once.

Then I have friends that I rarely see, but who are as precious to me as the ones that I see most often. They are people that I have known in the crossroads of my life, people who have taken me in in some way when I was hurt or afraid or broken or lost. People whose names remind me of tender meetings and precious moments in my life. I have two friends in California, people Bob and I went through seminary with, people who let me come and see them once every few years or so when I need to get away. We go for months and months, years usually, without seeing or talking to one another and then spend a week together as though we had never been apart.

Then there are the friends who are way past just being friends, buddies is a better term maybe. The ones you talk to almost all the time, the ones you take trips with and raise kids with and buy birthday gifts for. The ones who know everything about you and like you anyway. The ones who know about your good points and your bad points, the ones who know your secrets and your hopes. The ones who bring you soup when you are sick and bring you presents when they come back from vacation.

I know enough about me to know that one of the reasons that I have a lot of friends is because I haven't ever met any strangers. I also know that some of us are a good bit more shy and retiring than others and can count their friends on their two hands. Maybe. I am coming to believe that most of us have more friends than we let on.

I am also coming to believe another thing about our friendships. No matter what else has gone into our meeting and knowing each other, what holds us together is the stories that we tell each other and the stories we actually live out together, the ones we hold dear and remember and retell and revisit.

Stories, and the art of remembering and retelling them, were always a big deal at our house. It was probably Bob who made that so for us, and it was one of the most important gifts he left us.

Another great gift he left us was the gift of his own stories, the ones he told to us and the ones he told on countless platforms and stages across the country. They were the stories of his family and co-workers that we had known and loved. They were stories of his friends and acquaintances that we had only met through the telling of the stories. They had appeared in his books and on his tapes, and they were foremost among the things that bound us to those who had known him.

As time went by, we came to see that we had first been given those stories as a gift on the occasion that we first heard them. Now that they had been left to us in a different way, in the form of manuscripts and copyrights, we felt they were a gift that we could not keep to ourselves, but rather one that should be given away again. They were not meant to be clutched tightly in our hands, but to be shared.

Within a few weeks, the idea of collecting his best stories into one book had begun to take shape. When we had sold all the copies that we had and were getting ready to publish them again, a new friend of ours who was helping us to put them out asked us what the stories had come to mean to us in the time that had gone by since Bob had passed away. For one of the few times in my life, I was almost speechless. For most of my life, that wasn't even my kind of question. It was the kind of question that in times gone by I would have passed to my partner, the poet, for an answer.

Not too long ago, I heard a man named Bob Conn give a talk about the parables. One of the things he said was that most of us don't see our lives as stories, though we should. In fact, he said, if we would take more time to see our stories and tell our stories and listen to the stories of others, we would come a lot closer to understanding the value that is in our lives.

He reminded me that the story of my life is in those stories that Bob told. And not just in the ones that are about me or my children or my house, but in all of them in a way. When I read them, I can see the faces and the rooms and the beaches and the trips and the trees and the houses and the hands that made those stories real. I can see the faces of people that I have met and known and loved and cared about. And I can see the places that we met, for the first time or the last time. And I can see that life is full of stories that show that God is alive and well and working in our world.

❦

When I was working in the flower shop, I kept hearing Bob's stories, and my stories and the stories my friends would tell, saying that if I wasn't careful I would miss some more of the stories that were there to hear and to be told. That there were children and grandchildren who were growing up, and that if I didn't spend some time with them, I would miss them. And if I didn't hear some stories and pass them on, some of them would go unnoticed. And then too, someone would call or write or come to town for a visit, and I would remember their stories and think to myself, "I wonder what has happened since...."

So I began to commit myself to listening to stories and telling stories and looking for new ones to tell. I know it doesn't sound like much of a job description, but it is turning out to be pretty good work.

❦

These days I have another place that I make friends, I make them when I travel and speak. I remember them because of their stories.

When people first began to call to ask me if I would be willing to come and speak to their group, I hesitated. I was always happy to have a little trip, but I wasn't sure that I really had anything to say. I worried some about whether or not I would be able to talk about Bob without breaking up or breaking down. I worried about whether or not people would think I was doing it for the right reasons. I worried about whether or not people would be disappointed that I wasn't as good a storyteller or as smart as he was.

When we were raising our kids, we always took a great deal of pride in the fact that there weren't any two alike. We thought it was right to let them go their own way, to find their own talents and interests without being bothered too much by trying to be like each other or like us.

181

At the high school where three of our kids attended, there was a geometry teacher named Mr. Fisher. He was one of Robert's favorites, though not because Robert had a passion for geometry. It turned out that if you were a basketball player and did your homework and if it was right, you could get out of class early and go to the gym. Well, Robert was and so he did and went to the gym. Michael wasn't a basketball player, and he also wasn't a big fan of geometry, so that when he went through Mr. Fisher's class, Mr. Fisher didn't have the same regard for him as he did Robert.

On one occasion, he sent a note home with Michael's report card that indicated Michael had been doing less than he should have. We saw Mr. Fisher that evening taking tickets at the football game. So I told him who I was and that we had seen the note and would be talking with Michael to get it straightened out. I don't remember everything he said about Michael, but I do remember him saying, "Well, I can tell you one thing. He's no Robert." He didn't realize that he had ended our conversation on such a high note for me and Bob.

I finally began to hear that I am only called to be me. That even though I am no scholar, and maybe no great shakes as a storyteller either, certainly not like Bob and some others that I know, I do know some stories and I do know that stories need to be told.

I have come to see that there are stories out

there somewhere that are waiting to be told and heard. The world is full of stories of love and sacrifice and courage and the way God works in the lives of people. Stories of courage and hope, of pain and determination, of defeat and grace. Stories that are the very fabric of the tapestry that binds God's children to each other. I know it's true because I hear the stories all the time. Only the names and the cities are different.

So now I travel and talk a little about Bob's stories and my stories and some others that I have heard. People seem to like it and they are as kind to me as they were to Bob. I'm easier to get along with in a way, because I can make small talk at the dinner table, and I will eat their casseroles and he couldn't. And we swap stories and if they are shy about telling me theirs, I keep talking to them until they do. I'm a mom, I know how to get people to talk about themselves.

I have begun to believe that my work and Bob's work are the same. In fact, one way or another, it may be the work that all of us are to be about. Stories like these are the way that God uses his children to tell his story to his children.

❧

I was somewhere not too long ago and noticed a flower arrangement on a table. It was breathtaking.

It was in a small vase, about six inches high. It had a few orchids, a few somethings I couldn't identify, and a few long blades of a wild grass of some sort. It was pretty small actually, but it had a character about it that caught my eye. Though it was small, it seemed to occupy a space that was larger than itself. When I asked, someone told me that it had come from the shop where I had worked.

I smiled to myself and thought of something they had taught me there about arranging flowers. The thing to do is to let each flower have its own air and space, to give each one enough room to be itself. When you have done that, you have made a place where each one can contribute to the whole. And then, put them out where they can be seen, where their presence can be felt, where their life can show.

It's the thing to do with stories too. Give them air and space and then put them out there. Out where they can be heard, where their presence can be felt, where their life can show.

Go to Weddings

❦

Of this I am confident,
that he who started the good work in you
will bring it to completion by the
day of Christ Jesus.

PHILIPPIANS 1: 6

❦

LEIGH AND I had planned her wedding off and on for about twelve years. There were a few holes in the plan, like a groom and a wedding date, but it didn't keep us from going ahead with the planning. When a mother has four boys and one girl, it sinks in pretty quick that she is only going to get one shot at such an event, and so she prepares early and often.

Our thinking had pretty much been all along that we would have a long time to plan the actual details once the groom and date questions were settled. The seamstress would have about a year to make the dress, and we would have months and months to plan the guest list and line up the bridesmaids and choose the flowers.

The actual answer to the groom question showed up rather unexpectedly one evening on the first and last blind date of Leigh's life. And not too many weeks later, the date question got answered too. The wedding we had been planning for twelve years was going to take place in about twelve weeks. Quickly realizing that our initial plan to have the Queen of England attend was going to run into some scheduling difficulties, we proceeded to make new plans as though this whole idea of a wedding for Leigh was one we had never thought of before.

Most of our lives don't work out the way most of us plan.

I planned to be married to Bob Benson forever. But it didn't turn out that way. And I had pretty much planned to be a housewife and homebody right up until the end of it too. If you had asked me a long time ago, I would have said that I would probably live in the house by the lake forever. I had a church to go to, and a circle of friends to knock around with, and a set of things to care about, and a fair amount of other stuff to go and do.

I had a way of thinking about my life and about God and about my children and my very being that was pretty comfortable.

And then it all changed. All of it.

❦

An hour or so before the wedding, we had everything we needed except a bride.

There were fine musicians, turned out in tuxedos, arranged in the sort of half circle that chamber musicians sit in, ready to play Pachabel's Canon and the other pieces Tommy had picked out. One of the advantages to marrying a serious musician is that you have great music at the wedding and great musicians to play it. The other advantage is that the wedding proposal comes wrapped in a piano suite that has been composed in your honor, a melody written only for you. When Leigh let me hear the piano suite one afternoon, I wasn't sure how long it would be before they were married, but I knew that the die had been cast.

There was a great cast of characters arranged as well. There were four brothers and a nephew, two ministers in long black robes, and a great host of bridesmaids and groomsmen all dressed up looking like the crowd that Cinderella had gone through on the night she lost a slipper and found a prince. When she was growing up, Leigh and I used to laugh about whether she could overcome her shyness enough to have a bridesmaid at all, and now she had enough for a ball.

With the possible exception of a certain Christmas Eve that I remember, West End Church had never looked finer. Great stands of flowers and candles, bursting with fragrance and light, called us to worship and celebration inside the house of the Lord. The afternoon sun, ordered up years in advance for this day, came through the stained glass and and took away the shadows and the chill from the great stone columns.

There were mothers-in-law in new dresses, and grandmothers in new hats, and cousins and nieces and nephews in new suits and dresses and such. There was an anxious father-in-law-to-be in his best man finery, and a great host of friends and the assorted hangers-on that one gets on a perfect wedding day. I have lived in towns with less people in them.

It was going to be a fine day as soon as we found a bride.

❦

All of these places I have been.

Could it be that in all of them, through all of them, that God has been speaking to me?

When I finally stopped to listen to his voice, was it possible that he had been whispering to me all along? Had he been in the check-out line and the nursery and the little one-room parsonage and the carpool and the hospital? Had he been at the dinner table and in the airport and down by the lake and over next door with me? Had I been making a home for him in me all this time and didn't know it?

Like a girl who hears a piano suite just for her and suddenly knows the answer to another question, I am beginning to hear that the answer to all those questions is yes.

I am hearing that there is no distance between the person that I have been and the person that he is calling me to be. A difference between those two, perhaps, but no distance. I have never not been the person that he has chosen. Neither have any of us.

The question seems to be whether or not we have heard him, or will hear him.

All our lives he is shaping us, loving us, calling us, being with us so that he can be at home in us. In all our bright celebrations and deep disappointments, all our shining moments and dark days, all our victories and defeats, he is there. Whispering, calling, shaping, loving.

Nothing in our lives, nothing that is our life, is apart from him or ever has been or ever will be.

❧

When I saw Leigh come through the parking lot, I was a little nervous. She was wearing her hose and sweatpants and tennis shoes and an oversized shirt that had obviously been liberated from the hairdresser's.

It turned out that she had gone to have her nails and her makeup and her hair done that morning, and upon discovering that if she wore her sweatshirt while she got her hair done, she wouldn't be able to pull it off over her head afterwards. It also turned out that she could walk up the stairs, into the room where the nervous dressmaker was waiting, and step into her dress. In a matter of a moment or two, she went from being the person who was most likely to be late to being the only female member of the wedding party who was actually ready for the wedding.

In the moment when Leigh turned around to face us, in the turning, she became the bride. Face shining, smile glowing, eyes sparkling, all with the anticipation of the celebration that was to come next. I have seen this girl a lot through the years and I had never seen more joy in her face than I did at that moment. Everything about her seemed to speak of the joy and anticipation and excitement she felt at going into her new life.

The moment only lasted for a moment, and then there were great shrieks of laughter as everyone in the room realized Leigh was the only one ready for the wedding. And during the great hustle and bustle that arose as a small squad of bridesmaids and attendants piled into their dresses and shoes, she slipped away again.

It turns out that she really didn't mean to go

into the sanctuary, it just sort of happened.

She had started out to go and find her brothers. She's been a sister long enough to know that it isn't very often you find your brothers all dressed up at the same time. They were having their pictures made out in the courtyard. So she watched the picture making for a while and posed with them all for a photograph or two.

Then she went around to the front of the church and talked with the musicians for a few minutes, and then she went down to the hall where the reception was being prepared to talk to the caterers and the punch ladies. Then she started running into people in the halls.

She thought that while she was out, it would be a good trick to peek inside the back door to hear the music, and when she saw her friends she couldn't resist going in. Before she knew it, she was working the room pretty good. Now working the room isn't something that Leigh always does, being the shy, retiring sort that she is. I know about working a room, I can evermore work a room.

She just started up the center aisle, talking and greeting and laughing and hugging and smiling and remembering. I am pretty sure that I have never seen such a thing at a wedding before, and I am reasonably certain that some of the folks that Leigh was kissing and hugging and waving to hadn't either. Now that I have seen it once, I wish it was something that I saw at weddings all the time.

She told me later that she went for the walk around the church because she didn't want to miss her wedding day.

❧

I think there are times when all little boys want to be like their daddies. And I suspect there is a time when all little girls want to be like their moms. As time goes by and kids grow up, other heroes and heroines come on the scene, and children try those on one at a time, until one day they discover that what they most want to be is themselves. It has finally happened to me too.

What I want to be more than anything these days is to be Peggy. I'd even like to be a better than average Peggy if I could. But if I can't, a "just" Peggy will do. I want to live her life and sing her songs and dance her steps and tell her stories. All of it, the good and the bad and the mundane and the holy. And I want to do it with the face Leigh wore on her wedding day. Or one as near like it as I can muster.

❧

How many of our days do we miss, I wonder?

There are some days that go by so fast that they are a blur. Whole weeks and months worth of them sometimes. Days that get so full of all the things that there are to do that there is no time to notice the days as they pass, much less think about them.

There are days of celebration and grief and achievement that change our lives forever, and yet we can hardly remember them sometimes. There are days when holy moments have come to us, and later we discover that we are living our lives as though those moments had hardly happened to us at all. The times we do think about them, we wonder why they don't come again.

There are stories we live out that we can't recall and conversations we have had that we can't remember. Some of them happened yesterday and some the day before.

There are days we sit in the house of the Lord and forget whose house we are in or why we are even there. We get lost in all the trappings of the gathering and forget the Host. We remember the dance but forget the music. We go to the ceremony but miss the wedding.

There are times we sit with the ones we love, in circles that are sweet and familiar, and forget that, as much as anywhere else we will ever be on earth, this is the place where we will find God. That these are the places and the times where we will see his grace and light and love and truth. And that these friends are the ones who will show it to us.

Somehow, all that has to change for us. Somehow, we have to learn to pay better attention to the stories we are living and the moments we are making. Somehow we have to find some time to stop and see what is happening to us and in us and around us, in our own lives and the lives of the ones we know and love. We cannot let the busyness of our lives keep us from actually living them.

We have to find some time to be still and see the grace that surrounds us, to be open to the touch of the hand that is leading us. We have to find the time to listen to the voice of the God who whispers.

Epilogue

❦

Well I know
that I shall see the goodness of the Lord
in the land of the living.
Wait for the Lord;
be strong and brave,
and put your hope in the Lord.

PSALM 27:13, 14

❦

AT Christmas time, the first year after Bob died, I had a little trouble getting into the holiday spirit.

The time drew near and you could see the lights on the trees in the windows of the houses on my street. At first those lights made me sad. After a while I got to where I enjoyed seeing them, they reminded me that somewhere there was light and warmth and hope and laughter and joy.

A few blocks away, on the corner, the Boy Scouts had the Christmas tree sale working just as hard as ever, and a few more blocks away, at the mall, the shoppers were in full swing. I seemed to be able to manage the shopping. It was easy to buy for my children and for my grandchildren, thinking of their faces being so full of joy on Christmas morning must have helped.

But I couldn't seem to quite get in the mood for decorating the house. No tree seemed like the right one, even though I hadn't really looked. And the kids, responding to my muttering about "maybe we should have Christmas dinner at someone else's house this year" had made plans to do just that. I did manage to land an invitation.

Then the rumor got around that I wasn't even going to have a tree. According to them, that was going too far.

They all just showed up one afternoon. Tom had gone to find a tree, bringing it home to my house in the back of his pickup truck, and hauling it up the back stairs on his back. The rest of them started stringing the lights and laying out the food, and somebody headed for the stereo to put on the Andy Williams Christmas album, the one I have been listening to for twenty years.

It took a while, but before too long I was humming the songs and working my way through the cheese ball and teasing the grandkids about their presents.

❦

The next year at Christmas time, the kids said, "Well, Mom, so what day are we going to come and decorate your house?" And I said, "Well, I think I might do it myself this year," and they took that as a good sign of some sort and left me to it.

But the time kept getting closer and the house kept looking emptier and I kept getting sadder and not much got done. It was starting to look like there wasn't to be much of a tree or anything else at my house.

One evening I got a phone call from Amy Gaither. She had just started college in Nashville and she was feeling a little forlorn about the fact that at Bill and Gloria's house the Christmas season was in full swing, and down here in Nashville, for her at least, it was hardly moving along at all. It was the first Christmas that she hadn't been at home to help with the tree. Since we were both homesick, we decided to do my tree together.

So Amy came and between the two of us one evening, we got the house decorated.

When my kids came around in the next few days, they were pretty much impressed with how festive I was managing to be. After a while, I told them the truth, that it was mostly Amy's fault.

❦

The next year, the season came around again and for some reason I was ready for it.

By the time some of the kids dropped by to say, "Well, Mom, when are we going to decorate?"

the living room was already fairly glowing.

One night, I had dragged out the Andy Williams record, lit a few candles for atmosphere, and charged into it. I hauled the tree home in my trunk, brought up the lights and the decorations from the garage, and had at it. Around midnight, I turned off all the lights except the ones on the tree, sat down in the chair in the corner, turned up the music, and read a Christmas story or two to myself. It had been a long trip from the lights of the harbor in Nantucket to the lights from the tree in the corner of my living room.

A voice I had come to listen to and to trust said, "Light the lights. Let the music begin."

❦

There are times in your life when you don't feel much like celebrating at all. Times when, if there is to be any joy and light and warmth, then someone may have to bring it in the front door with them.

But there are also times when you find that you just cannot hold the joy in any longer. When it wells up inside you and spills out into your living room and through your hall and out onto the floor.

I think those are the times when it is a good idea to draw back your curtains. Someone may be passing by on the street in the dark.

❦ ABOUT THE AUTHOR.

Peggy Benson is a warm, openhearted lady with a ready smile and a deep interest in people everywhere, enabling her to live a life virtually devoid of strangers. Local shopkeepers, small children, and growing audiences all fall equally under her spell.

While she claims she is not a public person—insisting she has *only* been a housewife and mother—her influence has been felt wherever she goes. She has been a friend and confidante to artists, writers, pastors, and publishers all over the country.

Behind her bright smile and shining eyes is the gentle strength, warm heart, special sensitivity, and quiet confidence of an extraordinary woman, parent, and friend.

She lives in a Nashville home, visited frequently and cheerfully by the five children raised by her and her late husband, Bob Benson, the noted author, publisher, and speaker.

This is her first published work.

❦ ABOUT GENEROUX, INC.

Generoux is a small Christian press formed to create platforms for uniquely gifted writers and speakers who might otherwise go unpublished and unheard. The company takes its name from the French word that means *openhandedness*, a favorite theme of its founding spirit, Bob Benson. For more information about Generoux, its writers, publications, and retreats, please write to Post Office Box 158531, Nashville, Tennessee 37215 or telephone 615.889.8306.